GUIDED
IMAGERY *for*
GROUPS

Fifty Visualizations

that promote RELAXATION,

PROBLEM-SOLVING,

CREATIVITY, *and* WELL-BEING

GUIDED IMAGERY *for* GROUPS

Handwritten: 150401

Fifty Visualizations

that promote RELAXATION, PROBLEM-SOLVING, CREATIVITY, *and* WELL-BEING

ANDREW E. SCHWARTZ

Whole Person Associates Inc
Duluth, Minnesota

Whole Person Associates Inc
210 West Michigan
Duluth Minnesota 55802-1908
218/727-0500

Guided Imagery for Groups
Fifty Visualizations that Promote Relaxation,
Problem-Solving, Creativity, and Well-Being

Printed in the United States of America by Versa Press
10 9 8 7 6 5 4

Photographs by Darcy Dziedzic
Book Designer: Sally Rauschenfels
Editorial Direction: Nancy Loving Tubesing, Sandy Stewart Christian

Library of Congress Cataloging-in-Publication Data

Schwartz, Andrew E.
    Guided imagery for groups : fifty visualizations that promote
relaxation, problem-solving, creativity, and well-being / by Andrew E.
Schwartz.
    240 p. 23 cm.
    Includes bibliographical references.
    ISBN 1-57025-066-9 : $24.95
    1. Imagery (Psychology) 2. Imagery (Psychology)—Problems,
exercises, etc. 3. Visualization. 4. Meditation. 5. Self-actualiza-
tion (Psychology) I. Title.
    BF367.S36 1995
    153.3'2-dc20   94-42230
                                                          CIP

To the strongest images and influences in my life:
My Family
With Love and Light!

ANDREW E. SCHWARTZ

Andrew E. Schwartz is president of A.E. Schwartz & Associates, a management and employee development training and consulting organization based in Watertown, Massachusetts, that offers over forty training programs and practical solutions to organizational problems. Andrew conducts over one hundred fifty training programs annually, worldwide. At numerous business conferences he serves as a keynote speaker/presenter/ facilitator with a practical, succinct, and enjoyable style. Andrew also maintains a small, private practice in hypnotherapy. He founded the Training Consortium ™ , a national network and referral service that matches trainers with organizations.

Andrew is the author of over two hundred articles on management, professional development, and training. His books and products include *Delegating Authority, Inquire Within, Career Essentials for Secretaries and Administrative Assistants* (tape series), *School for Managers* (tape series), *Creative Problem Solving* (workbook/tape series), and *Stress Management.* Upcoming books include *A Training for Trainer's Handbook, Working with Groups in the Workplace: Time Management,* and *The Performance Management System.* Andrew has also reviewed and developed fourteen titles for the American Management Association's *New Business Success Series.*

Andrew's professional background includes extensive research in human consciousness. He has held positions as director of Equinnox Holistic Health & Arts Center, manager of training (information services) at the Massachusetts Institute of Technology, training director for the Smaller Business Association of New England, and on-site training director for The Employers Association.

DARCY DZIEDZIC

Darcy Dziedzic is a Boston-based free-lance photographer with an extensive background in the fine arts. After receiving her BA/BS from the University of Connecticut, she continued her studies at the School of the Museum of Fine Arts in Boston. In addition to regular appearances in Boston publications, her work has been shown in the Boston Film Festival, Rochester Institute of Technology's Under Glass Media Festival, The American Film Institute/Sony Visions tour, and the Boston Museum of Fine Arts annual showings.

Acknowledgments

I would like to acknowledge and thank the practitioners of this realm for their vision, and my researchers and interns for their hard work. Special thanks to Jacques, Jason, Jennifer, Dina, Evan, Lisa, George, Carla, Peter, and the staff at Whole Person Associates Inc.

I would especially like to thank all who, through self-exploration, choose to change their lives, for their interest and insight.

Contents

Chapter 1

INTRODUCTION

Guided imagery is one of the most potent tools we have as individuals to manage stress, unleash our creativity, change our attitudes, set and reach goals, tap into our inner wisdom, relax, stimulate peak performance, and activate our natural healing powers.

Guided Imagery for Groups is a collection of visualizations which are formatted for easy use with groups. The book includes warm-up relaxation scripts and over fifty guided imagery scenarios which are organized into seven sections. Each section pertains to a different group objective, ranging from simple images that promote relaxation or creativity to complex visualizations that stimulate problem-solving or healing.

Guided imagery, as a teaching tool, is meant for individuals interested in probing specific issues in their lives, as well as those seeking relaxation, sensory awareness, or avenues for introspective exploration. The scripts in *Guided Imagery for Groups* span the spectrum so you can match the interests of different groups and individuals. The images are open and inviting, not controlling. In fact, these visualizations will guide students to a place where they have more control over their lives.

WHO IS THIS BOOK FOR?

This book is intended to help you and the people in your groups become more directed about using relaxation and imagery for stress management, well-being, problem-solving, and personal fulfillment.

Whether you are a corporate trainer, a chemical dependency counselor, a hospice nurse, a team leader, or a neophyte wellness coordinator, relaxation and imagery experiences will enhance your classes, workshops, and training sessions. Guided images are a superb way to get a group settled down after a break. Visualizations are a perfect medium for planning or goal-setting. Imagery is a natural prelude to brainstorming. Calming and centering are healthy stress managers in any setting. Try them!

First-time guided imagery leaders are likely to find that relaxation and guided imagery techniques are easier and more effective than they might have imagined—practical as well as mystical. These natural human skills can help you expand your understanding of the mind, explore its mysterious workings, and harness its enormous potential. The added richness of the group experience is a bonus.

If you are a newcomer to visualization, the choices may seem overwhelming. Don't panic. This book is laid out to help guide you through the process, with presentation outlines, complete scripts, and helpful hints along the way. Remember, this is a skill building adventure. Experiment! As you practice on your own, and with different groups and varying images, be sure to consult the Resources section for practical implementation ideas.

If you are already fluent in the language of guided imagery, I trust you will find stimulating ideas and refreshing new images for using visualization with groups.

GROUP DYNAMICS ENHANCE VISUALIZATION

Although guided imagery is very useful for an individual seeking personal exploration and enhancement, it is also highly suited for group use. Its very name implies the need for a guide: a facilitator who leads the process so participants can let their imaginations roam freely in response to the images.

Guided imagery with a group can be especially powerful. Not only does each individual benefit from the personal inner journey, comparing notes afterwards allows us to learn from each other's experience. Talking about a visualization usually deepens its meaning to the individual and heightens the sense of connection to others in their separate journeys.

The group acts as a witness to what we have discovered; it also acts as a catalyst. The synergy of a group is contagious and even during the process of reading the visualization script a palpable group energy is often generated, serving to heighten the imagery experience for everyone.

Beginners in imagery learn best in a group with a guide who can direct self-exploration. Group synergy and support hasten the learning process. Later, as skills and motivation increase, self-guided sessions are possible—although reflecting on the experience and sharing insights with others are still important.

ROLE OF THE LEADER/GUIDE

BE PREPARED. Whatever script you choose for a particular situation, be sure to involve yourself with the images personally before using them in a group setting. Start by practicing on your own. Record the script and then let the tape guide you through the visualization as if you were a participant. This will give you good feedback about your pacing and inflection. Jot down your insights, or fragments of your experience. Then answer the reflection questions and share your insights with someone. This will give you an idea of what your participants might experience.

The more comfortable you are with the images and possible responses, the easier it will be to guide a group through the script.

CHOOSE APPROPRIATE IMAGES. First identify the goal you would like to achieve through guided imagery. If you want to teach people how to calm down at the end of a stressful day, look in the Calming or Centering section for an appropriate script. If you want to lead people through an exploration of values or life purpose, look in the Clarity or Congruence section. If you want to help people work through past issues or relationships that are affecting them today, check out the Connectedness section. Guided imagery also makes an excellent segue to and from other content material.

Read through several visualizations with similar goals to find the one you think will fit the time frame, image system, and sophistication level of your group. Study the script carefully, then personalize it to your style and the group's needs by adding or eliminating warm-up information, enhancing the script with words and images that may be particularly meaningful to the group, and planning a processing activity that fits the risk level and expectations of the group.

CREATE A HEALTHY ENVIRONMENT. As a group leader you have the power to control the environment in which the group learns and works. For guided imagery, make sure you create an environment that is entirely permissive. There are no right or wrong ways to visualize.

Adults learn from experience, which means that your participants will know what environment suits them best. Your group environment must make room for all of these respective experience-based comfort zones. For instance, if one person would like the lights on, and another prefers them off, try both. If some relax better on the floor, make sure their space is comfortable. If the imagery would be enhanced by an outdoor setting, go on location—or at least see that your meeting room is well ventilated.

Always make sure the room is at a comfortable temperature and free from distractions. Nothing is more disruptive to the imaging process than intrusive sounds or interruptions. Physical comfort is also essential. Backaches, headaches, and even the common cold can interfere with the hypnotic procedures of visualization. Make every effort to minimize any physical discomfort your group members may have.

PREPARE THE GROUP WITH INFORMATION. In most groups you will find some people who are familiar with guided imagery and others who are complete newcomers. You may even encounter some folks who are hostile or anxious because of what they have heard about visualization. In most situations, giving information about the technique and clarifying the specific activities you will be using goes a long way toward alleviating resistance and getting the group on the same playing field.

Information in the Relaxation Basics and Guided Imagery Basics presentation outlines (Chapters 2 and 3) will provide a good starting point. Many scripts also have introductory material in chalktalk format for your use in preparing the group.

Encourage your participants to approach the guided imagery experience with an open attitude and a vacation mentality of exploration, fun, and discovery.

PREPARE THE GROUP WITH RELAXATION. Always begin a guided imagery session with some form of relaxation. Even a few deep breaths will help people calm down and turn their attention inward. Each script has a few lines of breathing and centering. For maximum benefit, and with complicated images, use a five to twenty-minute relaxation routine to help participants reach a truly altered state of consciousness before beginning the imaging process.

If you don't have a favorite relaxation routine of your own, you'll find relaxation scripts in Chapter 4 and additional techniques suggested in the Relaxation Basics Presentation, Chapter 2.

READ THE SCRIPT WITH AUTHENTIC STYLE. There is no one right way to read relaxation and guided imagery scripts. Some narrators use an expressionless monotone. Others infuse their reading with pacing and inflection intended to heighten the imagery. Some speak with strength and authority. Others barely whisper. You need to find your own natural style.

However, there is one essential guideline for reading: take your time. Remember that your listeners do not know what is coming. They need time for the mental images to form and unfold. They need time to explore and sense. They need time to make transitions.

Listen to some pre-recorded imagery tapes to find out what feels like a comfortable pace and voice to you. Practice matching that rhythm and expressiveness. Test out different styles by reading scripts to family and friends. Listen to their feedback—and to the feedback of your groups. When you find an authentic style that works for you and your audiences, stick to it!

■ FACILITATE PROCESSING OF IMAGES. It may seem risky or too personal to require participants to talk about their guided imagery experience. I believe the benefits far outweigh the risks. Affirming discoveries out loud powerfully reinforces new insights or decisions. Hearing others' stories triggers new insights. Don't miss this built-in learning enhancer.

Each script is followed by one or two reflection questions. Give people a chance to affirm their insights by saying them out loud to at least one other person. Individuals can choose the level of disclosure that fits them. And if it fits your goals, spend a significant amount of time in this rich activity.

■ LEARN FROM EXPERIENCE. These guidelines, like most of the contents in this book, are designed to be modified time and time again by you, the group leader, as you gain more experience with guided imagery in groups. Keep notes about each visualization experience, with suggestions for improvement or adaptation. Ask for feedback from your groups about what they find particularly valuable or meaningful. Continue to experiment so you can stretch and grow along with your participants. And have fun!

ORGANIZATION OF THE BOOK

The next two chapters of *Guided Imagery for Groups* are intended to give the leader content information and process ideas for teaching about relaxation and guided imagery.

Chapter 2 presents an **overview of relaxation techniques** that can be used effectively for personal enjoyment and stress management. Notes to the group leader *(in italics)* suggest experiential activities to demonstrate the concepts.

Chapter 3 outlines the **basic concepts of guided imagery** in chalktalk format, with suggestions to the leader for inserting imagery experiences to illustrate the presentation.

The scripts in *Guided Imagery for Groups* are loosely organized into eight chapters for your convenience. There is no magic in the groupings. The categories overlap, so be sure to look through them all if your group has a special need. The divider sections between chapters give a short capsule description of the visualizations in that section. The scripts are organized in each section from simple to more complex images.

Each visualization includes specific goals, timing techniques, hints for preparation, special considerations the leader may need to consider, warm-up concept chalktalks, reflection questions, and instructions for processing the experience in small or large groups.

Although all of the imagery scripts have a very brief relaxation component, for maximum benefit you will want to use one of the foundation **Relaxation** scripts in Chapter 4 as a prelude to group visualization.

Chapter 5, **Calming**, includes physical and mental images which help people release tension as they become calm and quiet.

Chapter 6, **Centering**, focuses on letting go of tension or anxiety, and returning to a state of harmony and balance.

Chapter 7, **Creativity**, helps people transform, release, and create new energy, new images, new places, and new processes, challenging them to break out of old patterns and make bold changes in life habits and directions.

Chapter 8, **Congruence**, includes images that are designed to help people develop self-awareness, self-acceptance, honesty, and integrity.

Chapter 9, **Clarity**, facilitates mental and spiritual clarity.

Chapter 10, **Coping**, guides people into new strategies for coping with stress, tension, emotional pain, illness, and disease.

Chapter 11, **Connectedness**, helps people reflect on the profound relationships they have with other people, nature, themselves, and the world.

Chapter 12, **Resources**, includes tips for group leaders. This how-to primer has ideas for preparing and enhancing images, maximizing the benefits of group dynamics in processing images, responding to resistance and emotional reactions, and working with an ongoing group or class.

The bibliography provides a good starting place for furthering your education about guided imagery. The final section highlights music for relaxation and imagery, including sources for some of the most effective recordings to use with groups.

Chapter 2

RELAXATION BASICS PRESENTATION

✏ *This outline walks you through a suggested sequence for teaching the principles of relaxation to your group. As with any teaching design, be sure to adapt it to your group and setting, personalizing the presentation with your own style and anecdotes.*

✏ *Since relaxation is an essential prelude to effective use of guided imagery, you may want to incorporate some or all of the information in this chalktalk as an introduction to visualization.*

✏ *The best way to learn about relaxation is to try it. In an extended course or workshop on relaxation, you might want to lead the group through several different types of relaxation sequences. Even if your time is short, you still need to provide one or two brief experiential learning opportunities.*

STRESS AND RELAXATION

▓ Stress is a fact of life: deadlines, juggling work and personal commitments, interruptions, rush hour traffic, conflict at home, or even the ringing of an alarm clock. Everyone knows the feeling of being under stress.

▓ The stress response is physical as well as perceptual or emotional. The body undergoes several powerful internal changes when we are under stress: adrenaline pours into the blood stream, preparing us to fight off the potential danger of the stressor; muscles throughout the body tense in anticipation of the challenge. Since the stressors we face these days are usually not the type we can physically fight or flee, we generate more muscle tension than we need in most situations.

Except in extremely stressful situations, such as a near-accident on the freeway or being called on to make an impromptu speech at a large gathering, we are usually unaware of the physical process of gearing up that accompanies stress. When we do nothing to discharge the tension, it accumulates, building up over the hours, days, and years. Most of us have conditioned ourselves to accept persistent muscle tension as "normal." We tend to notice our tension only when the pain level increases to the point where we can no longer ignore it.

▓ Relaxation is the body's natural antidote to stress. People who learn how to relax deeply can become aware of mounting tension and soothe it, before it festers into headaches, backaches, and other physical pains.

Relaxation provides an opportunity for the body to continually energize itself. It allows the body to become aware of its stressors and to produce a state in which the body can cope with them. Relaxation helps you to handle your stress, learn new concepts and behaviors, and maintain physical health.

WHAT IS RELAXATION?

▓ If you ask people what they do to relax, you are likely to get answers ranging from channel surfing to surf boarding, gardening, yoga, catnapping, or playing the cello.

⤳ Stop and ask the group for examples of what they do to relax. You might want to write the responses on news-

print and refer back to them as examples, where appropriate, during the rest of your presentation. Be sure to personalize the discussion with your own experience.

Many people will suggest passive relaxation experiences—lying on a beach, listening to music. Others will focus on more active relaxation *nirvanas*—physical exercise, painting, writing, fixing the sink, or dancing. Your ultimate relaxation could be anything from scuba diving to meditation to doing the laundry.

Most of us, however, have not learned some of the basic skills that would help us incorporate enough relaxation into our lives to counterbalance the unhealthy effects of stress. Relaxation is an essential skill, not a diversion. And we can all improve our skill level to help us manage stress in a healthier way. No one technique will work for every person, every time you need to relax. The more strategies we know, the more likely we are to use one.

THE MIND/BODY CONNECTION

The goal of relaxation is to release unnecessary muscle tension and quiet the mind. Relaxation can take many forms, ranging on a continuum from *body-focused* tension relief (breathing, stretching, massage, progressive relaxation), to *combination strategies* that integrate physical and mental approaches for relaxation (passive progressive relaxation, yoga, autogenics), to *mostly mental* techniques (meditation, guided imagery) that calm, center, or clarify.

From the whole person perspective, the mind and body can't be divided so neatly. The mind and body work together in harmony to bring about relaxation. Physical relaxation creates peace of mind as a by-product. Mental uncluttering slows down breathing and reduces tension. Integrated mind/body approaches can be particularly powerful.

All the different forms of relaxation are important because they appeal to different people and may be appropriate for different life situations. And they are all stress reducers. Let's look briefly at the variety of relaxation options, beginning with the *mostly physical* end of the continuum.

Body-Focused Techniques

▧ **Breathing.** The easiest body-only technique for relaxation is something you've been doing since your precipitous arrival in the world: breathing. Since we breathe unconsciously, most of us don't pay much attention to the process. Yet breathing is the key to relaxation for stress management. A yawn, a big breath, and a deep sigh provide instant stress relief. Sustained deep breathing can counteract the ill effects of the stress response.

> ↪ *Stop and insert a breathing experience here. Use the Quick Breath script from page 34 if you have time. Otherwise, try the simple yawn and sigh, inviting people to imagine they are blowing tension out of their body with every exhalation. Or introduce your favorite breathing technique.*

Breathing deeply stretches the muscles of the upper torso, while bringing increased oxygen to the bloodstream and increased capacity to expel wastes and release tension as we exhale. Since breathing is our natural tension-releaser, it is a powerful building block for all other forms of relaxation.

▧ **Stretching.** Stretching is another natural stress reliever. Properly stretching your muscles and tendons has numerous benefits, among them the achievement of a relaxed and peaceful state. When you stretch, the fibers of your muscles are separated slightly, allowing more blood to reach and revitalize each muscle cell. Your heart and respiratory rates slow down, your digestive tract resumes its coating function, and you are physically stable.

There are several different stretching techniques for each muscle of the body. For relaxation benefit, concentrate on the muscle groups where you feel stress and tension the most—usually the neck/upper body, the back, and the legs.

Never rush the stretching process. Hold each stretch for up to thirty seconds while breathing regularly and deeply. Start slowly. Extend your stretch to a point where you can feel the muscle itself slightly stretching. To avoid any physical stress, never stretch to the point of muscular discomfort.

⊂ Stop and ask people to scan their body for tension, focus on an area that feels tight, then gently stretch that muscle group for 30 seconds, breathing deeply, and imagining the tension blowing out with their breath.

■ **MASSAGE.** The gentle rubbing of forehead, face, and head at your desk, a deep-muscle, full-body manipulation at the health club, or a stimulation of acupressure points by a trained massage therapist are all excellent ways to help tense muscles let go and relax.

The relaxation effects of both massage and stretching can be enhanced by heat. Try a hot tub or heating pad to warm up your muscles beforehand. Everyone knows the magical restorative power of a long, hot bath.

■ **EXERCISE.** Physical exercise of any type is a double-barreled stress antidote. Exercise gives us a natural way to work off our accumulated tension—and we benefit from the rebound effect of relaxation that naturally follows exertion.

■ **SYSTEMATIC PROGRESSIVE RELAXATION.** Probably the most well-known relaxation technique involves the intentional tightening and release of every muscle in the body, one by one. Practice with this technique helps people become more aware of the sensations of tension, so they can tune into them more quickly and activate the relaxation response.

BODY/MIND TECHNIQUES

Yoga, passive progressive relaxation, and autogenic relaxation are three types of body/mind techniques that combine the strictly physical approaches with mental processes to enhance relaxation.

■ **YOGA.** The system of exercises and meditations we call yoga dates back eight thousand years. The purpose of yoga is to create a union of body, mind, and spirit.

The discipline of yoga focuses on developing three areas for optimal health. First, the physical body is strengthened through exercises to tone muscles, lubricate joints, increase flexibility, increase stamina, and develop vitality. Second, focused breathing creates chemical and emotional balance, and replaces negative emotions like anger and jealousy—which may cause illness—with positive emotions like joy, trust and love—which are associated with health. Third, the mind is focused on affirmations, which are similar to the power of prayer. The synthesis of these three powerful areas brings about a life harmony, which promotes health and healing.

PASSIVE PROGRESSIVE RELAXATION. Passive progressive relaxation uses the principle of systematically attending to tension in the various muscle groups of the body, but instead of using muscle contraction and release to achieve relaxation, you use mental imagery to visualize the tension draining away from the muscles.

Use the Passive Progressive Relaxation script from page 35 to demonstrate.

The first few experiences with this (and any) relaxation technique may not bring complete relaxation. As with any skill, it takes practice. So stick with it until you can relax deeply.

After several sessions, the routine will begin to feel comfortable, and you can adapt it to meet your own needs. You may need more time with one muscle group than with another. You may find more effective mental images for yourself. Or you may want to abbreviate the sequence for a quick relaxation break.

AUTOGENIC RELAXATION. Autogenic relaxation routines combine deep, rhythmic breathing with images of draining or melting tension away, rather than tightening and relaxing muscles. Autogenics use imagery to enhance sensations and promote circulation. Verbal statements, such as "my arms are warm and heavy," are repeated over and over as people concentrate on specific areas of their body.

Autogenic means self-produced, and many routines insert positive self-suggestions when in a deeply relaxed state. Specific problems such as smoking and overeating can be addressed with autogenic training, by using the basic techniques combined with verbal formulas that suggest control and mastery over the problem.

MIND-FOCUSED TECHNIQUES

Meditation and guided imagery are similar in style and intended outcome: both are strictly mental techniques which result in relaxation.

MEDITATION. Meditation has been practiced by people in religious contexts for five thousand years. Dr. Herbert Benson is responsible for identifying the relaxation benefits of meditative states and incorporating them into an effective secular technique he calls the "relaxation response."

Like autogenic strategies, meditation begins with a quiet environment, a passive, uncritical attitude, and rhythmic breathing. But the goal of meditation is to clear the mind—and then concentrate on a single mental focus (sound, image, object, phrase) for an extended period of time.

Meditation is not so much *doing* as it is *not doing* something, and learning to just *be*. The ability to concentrate in a relaxed, flowing, noncontrolling way is essential to the process. Benefits such as a lowered body metabolism, clarity of perception, alertness, renewal of energy, and a state of serenity are common.

GUIDED IMAGERY AND VISUALIZATION. Guided imagery capitalizes on the incredible capacity of the imagination to create and recreate sensory images that have a powerful impact on the mind and body.

↬ *Use this as a transition to the Guided Imagery Basics Presentation, page 26, or insert key points from the chalktalk.*

RELAXATION ENHANCEMENTS

ENVIRONMENT. Make sure the place you choose for relaxation is comfortable, warm, and free from distractions. Take the phone off the hook and dim the lights, if these help. Many people find an outdoor setting is ideal for relaxation.

TIMING. Experiment until you find the best time of day for relaxation. Perhaps you want to start the day with tranquillity. Perhaps lunchtime is the best time for your relaxation break.

DURATION. When you are learning a particular relaxation skill, it will probably take fifteen to thirty minutes to achieve a relaxed state. As your skill level increases, you may be able to relax more quickly. Different techniques may take more or less time. You are the best judge of how much time to spend.

▨ **MUSIC.** Many people enjoy musical accompaniment for relaxation. The point of any relaxation routine is to find your own internal music and rhythm, so make sure any external music enhances rather than interferes with that process.

▨ **DOZING.** Falling asleep is fine if you're at home or at the beach, but dozing is not so fine if you're driving or at your desk. Set an alarm or timer if you're likely to fall asleep. Do not use relaxation techniques behind the wheel.

▨ **LISTEN TO YOUR BODY.** If it is difficult to relax at first, don't give up! Stop your session, but try again later. You *will* learn to relax. Your body will respond progressively to each technique. It may take time and several relaxation sessions before you completely relax and feel ready to continue. Listen to yourself. How you feel will provide you with feedback on your progress.

With practice you will develop a greater control, which allows you to remain relaxed, yet conscious, during your relaxation session. In time you will discover and master an optimal point to maintain. For many it is the point just before sleep and just before awakening, called the "twilight" state of consciousness.

PERSONALIZING RELAXATION

▨ The *practice* of relaxation is never as simple as the *concept* of relaxation. It may be a simple thing to explain, yet to actually reap the benefits of relaxation demands more than an explanation. You will need to practice. As with any new skill, your first few relaxation attempts may not measure up to your hopes, though with practice you can learn to relax when you need to.

▨ Remember, just as there is no one way to decorate a room, there is no one right way to relax. Experiment. Try several different paths to relaxation, trusting that you know what works best for you. Feel free to adapt and modify the techniques, adding the personal touches that make relaxation easier and more likely to be part of a regular routine.

Like moving into a new room or a new house, the practice of relaxation may take a little getting used to. However, in time, you make the necessary changes, and the room becomes your own and your house becomes your home.

Chapter 3

GUIDED IMAGERY BASICS PRESENTATION

⇝ *Relaxation and guided imagery go hand in hand, so if you haven't used the entire Relaxation Basics Presentation, you may want to extract a few key points about relaxation to use as a warm-up to this presentation.*

⇝ *If you have time for an extended session on imagery, choose one or more brief scripts to use as guided imagery demonstrations at appropriate points during this presentation.*

⇝ *If your time is brief, just hit the key points in this outline and move directly to the visualization script of your choice.*

WHAT IS GUIDED IMAGERY?

Visualization is a process in which you use mental images to explore your inner psychic and creative space. You do it every day. When you wake up in the morning and think about what you have to do that day, you probably *picture* how these tasks will be done. When you realize that you must shop for groceries today, you inadvertently *picture* which ones you will need to buy. Lovers use imagery as they anticipate and recall the joys of being together. All of us daydream for entertainment.

Guided imagery takes this process one step further by *guiding* the images toward a specific life-enhancing goal, such as relaxing, healing, promoting personal growth, exploring alternatives, clarifying values, stimulating creativity, or managing stress.

Performers use imagery to heighten concentration. Managers use imagery as they plan strategies for tackling daily tasks. Diabetics use imagery to lower their blood sugar level. Athletes use imagery to enhance their performance. Cancer patients use imagery to bolster their immune responses.

SKILL, NOT MAGIC

Research is beginning to document the significant power of our mental processes to positively affect our well-being, yet guided imagery is not magic. It is not a panacea for all that ails us. It is no substitute for traditional physical or mental health care.

Your mind's eye is one of the most potent tools you have for triggering relaxation and promoting changes in attitude, perspective, or feelings. The effectiveness of guided imagery is grounded in the mind/body connection. As far as your body is concerned, sensory *images* have nearly the same impact as actual sensory *experiences.* Your body reacts physiologically to the imagined smell of baking bread in the same way it would to walking into a bakery. Mentally anticipating a fearful event can be just as frightening (or even more!) than the event itself.

Guided imagery offers an opportunity to harness the natural power of your imagination to work for physical and mental health. It is a skill which can grow more useful with regular practice.

ALWAYS BEGIN WITH RELAXATION

Placing your body and mind in a state of active relaxation is the best preparation for the use of guided imagery. You will find that relaxation is to guided imagery as a cone is to ice cream: without it, you've got no handle on the real thing. Relaxation must precede, interact with, and be enhanced by guided imagery.

The benefits of guided imagery are mainly mental in nature; however, preparing for visualization is both a mental and physical task. The mind must *be prepared* to be explored, expanded, enhanced, and enriched. Once you've cultivated the ability to relax in a completely natural way, you will be able to activate physical, emotional, mental, and even spiritual relaxation at will.

Some people use guided imagery every day as part of a regular relaxation or meditation ritual. Others may use imagery only occasionally for specific needs such as healing after a divorce, recovering from surgery, generating new ideas for a project, or coping with a particularly stressful day.

Ultimately, if you integrate guided imagery into your life, you will probably feel a greater power to reduce stress and direct your life in a positive direction.

MEDITATION AND GUIDED IMAGERY

People are often confused by the language used in relaxation and guided imagery training. The terms visualization and imagery are usually used interchangeably to refer to the active evocation of mental sensory images—sight, sound, taste, smell, and touch.

The term meditation is used to describe an altered state of consciousness that accesses what we call a vertical path of relaxation, advocated by many Eastern philosophies. By emptying your mind, focusing on a single visual cue, and using conscious, monotonous activities, such as repeated mantras, you can achieve a relaxation state similar to sleep, where your mind is disengaged.

Guided imagery, on the other hand, incorporates both a vertical and horizontal path of mental awareness to achieve a state of mental activity and creativity as well as relaxation. It allows for the more Western tendencies towards activity and controlled mental exploration.

With each image explored, in addition to relaxing vertically, you develop a pattern of lateral mental pathways. Exploring this pattern is entirely controlled by your conscious mind and does not resemble falling asleep. You may pause at one image, move on to another, revert back to the first one, or even explore a series of images at once. You may search this lattice of images as you please, always moving in an active pattern of imagination. A healthy dialogue is sustained by the conscious receptors of your brain and the unconscious explorations of your mind.

You Are in the Driver's Seat

By allowing for personal involvement and by adjusting with personal changes, imagery is exactly what you make of it. Of course, if you choose to be bored with the infinite reaches of your mind, you will be. If you are at all inquisitive and desire to find what lies beneath the surface, you will not be disappointed with your inner journey.

Guided imagery is not mind control. The visualization process actually gives control back to the individual, making conscious what has been an unconscious process and influence.

Imagery techniques allow for personal changes by changing and growing with you. The more adept you become at image exploration, the stronger your unconscious mind grows, and the more pathways you have at your command.

Be Open to the Process

Since guided imagery is a process of self-exploration by creating images of physical journeys and settings that reflect inner states and feelings, it is most effective when approached with a clear and open mind.

Let yourself go with the flow of the narration. Preconceptions lead to assumptions and expectations, which could prevent you from tapping into your natural stream-of-consciousness state.

Match your attitude to your goal

Unlocking your mind's experiences and images begins with a healthy approach to imagery. The attitude with which you enter and exit these experiences is the key ingredient of that approach.

When forming your attitude, keep in mind two general ideas: the intended outcome of this journey, and the practical means of achieving that outcome. For example, if you intend to use guided imagery as a significant turning point in your life and as a pathway to change, then your attitude must be conducive to change. If you are hoping to discover and unlock greater emotional or intellectual scope, your attitude must reflect boundlessness, an interest in pursuing all dimensions of your creativity and awareness. Always keep your intended outcome in mind, and choose your imagery exercises accordingly.

On the other hand, whatever your goal, it is essential to approach any guided imagery with an open mind.

PAY ATTENTION TO ALL YOUR SENSES

While guided imagery techniques will appeal most obviously to your sense of sight and your "mind's eye," don't miss the rich experience of your mind's other senses. What smells or tastes accompany the image in your mind? What internal or external sensations do you experience? What sounds can you hear?

All five of your senses are important channels for accessing hidden, forgotten, or undiscovered aspects of yourself, as well as for exploring new avenues and opportunities. Whenever you embark on a guided image, tune in to your senses.

NO WRIGHT, NO RONG

When choosing to immerse yourself in imagery exploration, there is, by definition, no right or wrong way to do it. You are the explorer, and the territory is all your own. You go where you want, when you want, with whatever supplies you need.

You are your own person, and have your own ways of relaxing and exploring. If an image feels uncomfortable, frightening, or just boring, tune it out for a while! Open your eyes if the visualization is too intense or painful for you. Feel free to follow your own visions as they surface. As long as you are comfortable, you cannot go wrong. Settle in, follow your instincts, and explore. Let your mind follow the path you choose.

And remember that the guided imagery experience will be different for every person. Take advantage of any opportunity to compare notes with fellow visualizers—someone else's journey may help you understand your own at a deeper level.

A NOTE OF CAUTION

Because everyone's life experiences are unique, it is very difficult to anticipate which images may trigger pain for certain people. Keep in mind that even though some guided images may be painful, they may be part of a healing process for past or present wounds. If possible, stay open to all your feelings, even painful ones, and allow yourself to experience them fully.

However, if you know in advance that a particular image might be frightening or emotionally upsetting to you, and you would prefer not to explore that arena, it is perfectly okay to sit out the exercise, or to modify the image in any way that you want.

■ Trust your intuition and do what is best for yourself.

DO-IT-YOURSELF IMAGERY

Most visualizations are open-ended, so you can project your own images and feelings into the mental landscape. If you find yourself enhancing the images with your own pictures and ideas, the techniques are working well for you.

■ With practice you can create your own images whenever you need them. But even people well-versed in the use of imagery still enjoy having a guide so they can surrender to the flow of the image and go wherever it takes them.

Try recorded visualizations with musical background, or read your own scripts and images onto tape and play them back.

■ The same guided imagery can be used over and over again, at different times of your life. Each time you revisit the same visualization, your experience will be different.

Chapter 4

SCRIPTS *for* PREPARATION

The two scripts in this chapter provide brief and extended relaxation routines that can be used alone for stress relief, or as a warm-up to any guided imagery script.

Quick Breath

Take a full, deep breath to generate relaxation.

GOAL

To relieve tension.

To prepare for deep relaxation or guided imagery.

TIME

1-2 minutes

WARMUP

Breathing is a powerful building block for relaxation. The quick breath technique can be used any time, any place, for instant centering and relaxation.

QUICK BREATH SCRIPT

The easiest body-only technique for relaxation is something you've been doing since your arrival in the world . . . breathing.
Everyone breathes, but few know how to breathe for relaxation.

Stop now, and take a truly relaxing breath . . .

Inhale through your nose with a shallow breath . . .
and exhale through your mouth . . .

Inhale slightly more . . . and exhale now with sound . . .

Inhale more deeply . . . and again, exhale forcefully . . .

Inhale to capacity . . .
and exhale completely, emptying your lungs all the way . . .

Repeat this breath cycle ten times . . .
or until you feel completely relaxed . . .
maintaining a steady rhythm of inhalations and exhalations as you breathe.

Passive Progressive Relaxation

*Experience the benefits of total-body relaxation
as you breathe deeply, improve circulation,
and find comfort, relief, and rest.*

GOAL

To relax deeply.

To prepare for guided imagery.

TIME

20 minutes

WARMUP

Passive progressive relaxation is a skill that emphasizes deep breathing techniques combined with imagery to create profound relaxation. You can master this skill of relaxation through practice and basic knowledge of your body's physiology.

Passive refers to the technique of *allowing* each area of your body to relax with your breathing and imaging, rather than the more *active* tensing and relaxing of muscle groups used in classic progressive relaxation techniques.

Passive progressive relaxation improves circulation throughout the body and provides significant benefits to other body systems. Improved circulation enhances the digestive process, speeding more nutrients to the body's cells. Deep breathing exercises your respiratory system, increasing the oxygen distribution to all parts of the body, and improving the disposal of waste from body tissues.

Passive progressive relaxation naturally calms the body and the mind, providing comfort, relief, and rest. This powerful relaxation process prepares you physically and mentally for guided imagery.

Once you learn the technique, you can easily adapt it to your personal images and rhythms.

During this exercise, you will be asked to take notice of how certain body parts feel at any given time. Pay particular attention to these sections! In fact, each time you are asked how something *feels,* try to put into words your sensations. For example, if you hear "take notice of how your legs feel," you might say *in your mind,* "Well, my ankles hurt a little on the sides. My calves feel just fine, but I can feel some pain on the backs of my thighs." Be that specific. Noticing tension or discomfort is as important as noticing relaxation.

Passive progressive relaxation works best when you are completely aware of your state of being, and tune in fully to the incremental process of progressively relaxing.

Remember, this is an exercise in *allowing,* not forcing. If your mind or body isn't tracking with the process or images, return your attention to your breathing and re-enter the flow of the script when you are ready.

PASSIVE PROGRESSIVE RELAXATION SCRIPT

Settle back comfortably . . .
and begin to focus on your breathing . . .
Take deep breaths in through your nose . . .
and exhale out of your mouth.

Continue to breathe in and out several times . . .
allowing the breath to come deeper and deeper . . .
from your lower lungs and diaphragm . . .
allowing any worries or concerns you may have . . .
to drift through your mind and out with your breath . . .
letting your breath clear your mind as you begin to relax.

⇜ *Pause 15 seconds.*

Begin to think about your body,
and its many different parts.

Pay attention to how each part of your body is feeling . . .
Does your back feel comfortable? Are your feet relaxed?

Is there noticeable pain anywhere in your body?
Just notice the sensations in your body,
without trying to change them.

Now, close your eyes . . .
and breathe in deeply through your nose . . .
bring the air all the way down into your diaphragm . . .
feeling your stomach rise . . .
letting the air move up into your lungs . . .
expanding your rib cage . . .

And now, exhale through your mouth.

Take another deep breath . . . in through your nose . . .
Notice how the air feels inside your lungs
as it gradually expands them from the bottom . . .
pushing the sides of your lungs out toward the wall of your
chest . . .
filling your lungs all the way to the very top under your collarbone,
fully exercising their capacity . . .

Exhale through your mouth.

Breathe several more times . . .
concentrating on the path that the air takes.

    ↶ *Pause 20 seconds.*

Inhale deeply again through your nose . . .
and focus on your feet.
Release the tension out of each heel . . .
Let all of the tension from the entire day flow out of your heels . . .
like air being released from a tire . . .

Perhaps today's stress and tension have made you feel like a heavy,
wet towel dumped on the floor . . . soaked with weight . . .

Imagine yourself lying flat, drying in the sun . . .
and letting your tension evaporate into the air around you.

    ↶ *Pause 5 seconds.*

Take another deep breath and turn your attention to your lower
legs . . . notice how they feel . . .

As this breath of air fills up your diaphragm
and moves into your lungs . . .
feel the blocked-up tension being released from your legs
along with the air of your breath.

If you detect any tension in your legs, inhale again . . .
and breathe it out.

    Pause 5 seconds.

Next, visualize your knees and upper legs . . .
Become aware of how they are feeling . . .
Notice any tension that is damming up the easy flow of relaxation
and exhale the tension away as you release your breath.

The pain in your compressed knee-joints responds to this new breath
of air, and escapes with it . . .

You can feel that your knees and upper legs
are now free from tension.

    Pause 5 seconds.

Now direct your breathing power to your hips and buttocks . . .
Do they feel locked and tight from sitting all day?
Loosen them up as you breathe deeply in through your nose.
Concentrate on each part, individually . . .
noticing the tension, allowing it to release as you exhale.

With each breath, all of your muscles, ligaments, and joints
will be loosened more and more . . .
as you allow yourself to sink further into the surface
your body is resting on.

    Pause 5 seconds.

Next, search for any discomfort
that you may find in your abdomen . . .
As your stomach rises slowly with another deep breath . . .
picture yourself floating easily in a calm lake . . .

While staying afloat, capture the tension in this breath . . .
bringing it up into your lungs . . .
and releasing it through your mouth . . .

Feel your abdomen relax and settle.

   ⌒ Pause 5 seconds.

Now approach the diaphragm and chest area . . .
Most of the tension has been released here already
as deep breaths of air have been traveling in and out . . .
yet faint remnants of stress may still remain . . .

Inhale, collecting these last traces of the hectic day . . .
and expel them through your mouth . . .
leaving your diaphragm, chest, and lungs clean and healthy.

   ⌒ Pause 5 seconds.

Now, turn your attention to your upper back,
shoulders, and neck . . .
The muscles here may feel a little distorted and tense . . .
from the strain of your posture . . .
Let them weigh heavy and sink you further into your support.

As the weight of your shoulders brings you down a few inches . . .
begin to concentrate on the joints in your shoulders.

As you inhale deeply again,
begin to feel these parts as light, lax, and free from tension . . .
Exhale away the stress that has made them tense
and locked all day long.

   ⌒ Pause 5 seconds.

Now move up to your head . . .
Let it become as loose as your neck and shoulders . . .
Let this light feeling encompass your entire head . . .
sinking you into another level of relaxation.

Shift now to your lower back . . .
Consider the pressure that has been focused onto your lumbar region
all day . . . sitting for long periods of time . . .
supporting the weight of your head, shoulders, and torso.

Now, imagine a small sun rising behind you . . .
warming each vertebra of your back
as it rises with your breathing . . .
As you breathe in deeply . . .

feel your spine warm and widen itself . . .
Feel it lengthen, and notice each vertebra decompress . . .

Exhale, and imagine moving your lower spine to the left and right,
exercising it and improving its mobility.

↶ *Pause 5 seconds.*

Now, become aware of your forehead and eyes . . .
Feel the lines on your forehead fade away as you exhale,
leaving it smooth and loose . . .

Let another breath fill your diaphragm . . .
and as you release it, let your eyes loosen from the stress
and sink further into relaxation . . .

Feel how loose each body part has become . . .
and let each sink a little bit further.

↶ *Pause 5 seconds.*

Now turn your attention to your arms and hands . . .
and picture a pot of water boiling . . .
Imagine your stress as steam, escaping from your body . . .

Inhale deeply . . . and as you exhale,
allow all of the steam to pass from your upper arm . . .
through your biceps . . .
down your elbow and your forearms . . . your wrists . . .
and out through your fingertips.

↶ *Pause 5 seconds.*

Become aware of your entire body.

Take another deep breath . . .
and enjoy its rejuvenating power as it clears all traces of tension . . .

Notice your jaw and teeth . . .
Feel your jaw relax as its tiny muscles become loose and tension-free.

Now that you are relaxed . . . remember this feeling!
Notice how it feels to be totally relaxed . . .

↶ *Pause 5 seconds.*

Notice how easily your blood is circulating . . .

how your entire body feels loose and clean . . .
Remember this feeling of calm.

The next time you feel tension mounting . . .
Take a deep breath and remember this feeling of calm . . .
allowing your body to relax as you anticipate oncoming stressors.

Practice recalling this feeling of peace and tranquility
whenever you need it.

Now, let yourself out of this deep state of relaxation gradually . . .
Continue your deep breathing as you move your fingers . . .
and wiggle your toes . . .

   Pause 5 seconds.

It is important not to force yourself out of this state . . .
so come out as slowly as you need to . . .

   Pause 5 seconds.

Whenever you are ready . . .
take a deep breath . . .
and open your eyes.

CLOSING CHALKTALK

Like any skill, relaxation takes practice. As your skill increases and you become familiar with the indicators of a relaxed state, feel free to experiment with the basic passive progressive relaxation routine, adapting it to your needs of the moment.

By devoting twenty to thirty minutes a day to this technique, you will reap the benefits of "deep muscle relaxation," a physiological state characterized by optimum blood flow, heart rate, and hormonal activity. In this relaxed state the physical benefits translate quickly to your personal life: meaningful personal relationships are enhanced, and your professional life continues at a productive, relaxed pace.

You may not notice results from deep relaxation until the end of the first or second week. Learning to relax is easy, but it requires time and practice. Although relaxation is a natural state of the human body, experiencing this feeling "at will" takes work.

Chapter 5

SCRIPTS *for* CALMING

The soothing sensory images in this chapter create a sense of contentment and calm. Participants reduce stress as they nurture the body, mind, and spirit through comforting touch and peaceful visualization.

The River

*Drift with the currents of a slow-moving river
as your tension floats away.*

GOAL
To release tension.

TIME
3–4 minutes

GUIDED IMAGE SCRIPT

Sit comfortably with your back straight . . .
Focus on your breathing . . .
notice your breath flowing in and out . . .
slowly and rhythmically . . .

As you focus on your breathing . . . close your eyes . . .
and continue to breathe slowly and deeply . . .
Gradually relax deeper and deeper.

↩ *Pause 10 seconds.*

You are relaxing . . .
and as you breathe slowly, deeply and naturally . . .
feel the chatter of your mind become calm and quiet.
Feel your mind become clear and spacious . . .
as spacious as the sky . . .
Your thoughts are like puffy clouds,
drifting in and out . . . in and out . . .
until finally, you have no thoughts left . . .
Your mind is clear and spacious . . . as you breathe deeply.

↩ *Pause 15 seconds.*

Your mind is free and clear . . . it is open . . . and empty . . .
There are no thoughts intruding in your mind . . .
as you listen to my voice . . .

It is your time to be quiet now . . .
time to be carried along with this daydream.

  Pause 10 seconds.

Imagine a deep, wide, slowly moving river . . .
Place yourself in the middle of the current . . .
peering up into the sky . . .
as if the water were holding you there motionless . . .

Feel the current moving slowly past your ears . . . neck . . .
chest . . . stomach . . . waist . . . legs . . . and feet . . .
so that you become part of the swaying current.

Hear the unique underwater sounds . . .
the water gently rolling over the rocks . . .
the sand rushing through the water . . .
and your legs swaying back and forth with the current.

As the water continues to support your body . . .
notice your tension releasing itself into the stream.
Concentrate not on staying afloat or staying in place . . .
but only on letting go of your body's tension . . .
and drifting with the current of the stream . . .
Feel how light your body is at this time . . .
how relaxed . . . how peaceful you feel.

Know that the very fact you have imagined your tension floating
away with the stream's current makes it possible and real . . .
Your tension has been released . . .
and you feel light and relaxed . . .
Tell yourself this now.

  Pause 5 seconds.

You will bring back this good feeling . . .
this feeling of lightness and relaxation.
When you are ready . . .
open your eyes slowly . . . and let in the sight of your surroundings.

GROUP PROCESSING OPTION

  Compare notes with other group members about how and when
you might use this image.

Candle Wax

Imagine your tension oozing away like
wax dripping from a burning candle.

GOAL

To become calm and centered.

TIME

3–5 minutes

SPECIAL CONSIDERATIONS

Quick, easy exercise to use at the beginning of any session to get the group relaxed and focused.

Especially appropriate for support or personal growth groups, yet neutral enough for the workplace.

GUIDED IMAGE SCRIPT

It's daydreaming time. Time to relax in peace and quiet . . .
Time to clear your mind of clutter . . .
and focus on images that will calm and soothe you.

As you begin to slow down and relax, gently close your eyes . . .
and turn your attention inward . . .
Notice your breathing and the surfaces that support you.

Notice the thoughts and images that cross your mind . . .
then let them drift as you clear your mental landscape.

As you continue to relax deeper and deeper . . .
imagine yourself in a dark, quiet room . . .
A candle is set on a table in the center of the room.

Imagine yourself striking a match and lighting the candle . . .
then blowing out the match.

 ⤺ *Pause 5 seconds.*

Focus your attention on the candle
as the initial smoke from the wick flickers up into the air . . .

The blue flame creeps slowly downward,
towards the melting wax . . .
creating a small pool of liquid on the top of the candlestick . . .

As the wick burns, this pool slowly becomes too large for the space
holding it . . . and it starts to overflow . . . much like the tension
stored in your body . . . that builds up and seeks release . . .

    ↩ *Pause 5 seconds.*

As you continue to watch your candle, the first drop of melted wax
escapes the lip of the pool . . . and slides down the side . . .

Then another drop slides down . . . and another . . .
followed by a slow, steady stream of melted wax . . .
escaping . . . dripping . . . sliding.

    ↩ *Pause 5 seconds.*

Now, imagine that the melting wax
is the tension in your mind and body . . .
melting . . . oozing . . . escaping . . . dripping . . . sliding . . .
finding its own release.

    ↩ *Pause 10 seconds.*

When you are ready . . . blow out the candle, and return your focus
to the present moment . . . and to your surroundings.

Now open your eyes . . . bringing back with you a sense of release
and calm from the melting candle.

GROUP PROCESSING OPTION

▨ Pair up with a neighbor and describe your experience during this
imaging.

HOMEWORK

▨ Invite participants to repeat this visualization at home, using a
real candle.

Melting Lake

*Relax into the warm waters of a lake as the
spring thaw melts away the ice.*

GOAL

To become focused and calm.

TIME

2–3 minutes

SPECIAL CONSIDERATIONS

Useful for any class or workshop on stress management.

GUIDED IMAGE SCRIPT

To begin, just feel the surface upon which your body rests . . .
Allow this surface to support you completely . . .

As you rest securely in your surroundings, feel your body giving way
gently to relaxation . . . ever so slowly and gently . . .
Allow yourself to relax and your eyes to close . . .

    ↬ *Pause 5 seconds.*

Focus now on any remaining tension in your body . . .
and think of your tension as a sheet of ice covering a lake . . .

The cold, frozen surface blocks you from feeling the warmth and
energy within you . . .

    ↬ *Pause 5 seconds.*

As the warm days of spring pass,
in your mind the ice begins to soften and melt . . .
and as the sun's warmth increases . . .
the ice begins to recede from the shore . . .

The icy-cold water becomes free of its rigid covering . . .
and begins to loosen and relax
as it soaks up the warmth of the sun . . .

Pause 5 seconds.

Feel your own icy tension recede and melt away . . .
leaving a warm, calm relaxed body of water . . .
open to the sun's soothing rays.

Pause 15 seconds.

You are relaxed and refreshed . . .
and in a moment you will open your eyes . . .

Pause 5 seconds.

As you feel this warmth spread, prepare to awaken
completely . . .
bringing back a feeling of relaxation and refreshment.

Recall the free, flowing movement of the open water . . .
and notice your steady breathing . . .
and the free flowing of your mind as you begin to awaken . . .

Take a few moments now to enjoy how relaxed and refreshed you
feel . . . and then open your eyes.

GROUP PROCESSING OPTION

Reflect on specific things you can do to keep your internal lake
warm.

Share your insights with a partner or small group.

Avalanche

Listen to the silence of a snowy field
where all is serene and quiet.

GOAL

To become calm.

TIME

2-3 minutes

SPECIAL CONSIDERATIONS

Could be used in the workplace as part of a discussion on the role of calm and quiet in reducing work stress.

WARMUP

The concepts of seeing darkness and listening to silence are very eastern thoughts. Their utility in our culture can be very calming influences.

GUIDED IMAGE SCRIPT

Concentrate on your breathing . . .
with each breath feel your body expand and contract . . .

⌒ *Pause 5 seconds.*

As you let go of each breath . . .
your mind begins to clear and your body lets go of its tension . . .
allowing your thoughts and body to come to complete stillness . . .

You are quiet . . . tranquil . . . and serene . . .

Allow your eyes to close as you feel these sensations.

⌒ *Pause 10 seconds.*

As you experience feeling quiet and calm . . .
a sense of purification begins to develop . . .

Allow yourself to drift into a deeper state of relaxation . . .
breathing deeply and allowing your imagination to roam until you
find yourself walking in a winter forest.

⮑ *Pause 10 seconds.*

You are walking in a forest . . . where everything is blanketed by
soft, white snow from a recent snowfall . . .

As you walk on this snowy path, you slowly emerge from the trees
into a large, open, snowy field . . .

In the far distance is a snow-covered mountain . . .
with a sheer cliff face . . .
Suddenly, near the top of the mountain . . .
a large section of snow slides off of the cliff and falls . . .
Thundering down the slope
until it eventually ends in a huge puff of white . . .

In the aftermath of the avalanche . . .
all is silent . . . nothing stirs . . .
the snowy field and mountain are completely quiet and calm . . .
Allow yourself to enjoy the stillness . . .

⮑ *Pause 10 seconds.*

This stillness . . . and serenity . . . and purity . . .
is a pleasant feeling to experience and bring back with you . . .

Focus on this feeling of serenity as you begin to become aware of
your body in its present surroundings . . .

As you consciously become aware of your breathing and my voice,
allow yourself to gently open your eyes as I count to three . . .
returning to the room with this sense of calm and refreshment.

Awakening and returning now . . . one . . . two . . . three . . .

GROUP PROCESSING OPTION

▧ Think of other winter sounds that are soothing to you.

▧ Spend a few minutes talking with your group about
relaxing sounds.

Foot Massage

Smooth away tension with a calming, nourishing touch.

GOAL

To relieve stress.

TIME

5 minutes

SPECIAL CONSIDERATIONS

This activity could be used as a playful warm-up for informal groups in a stress management or wellness program, but it is probably not appropriate for most work settings. People might prefer to do the foot massage alone, at home.

WARMUP

After a stressful day spent on your feet, massaging the soles and tendons of the feet can be extremely relaxing. It may also be health-enhancing.

Oriental medicine identifies specific areas of the feet that are physiologically connected by energy pathways to each organ system of the body. Stimulating these points helps maintain the balance and healthy functioning of the associated body systems.

Before we begin this stress break, let's prepare our feet.

Remove your shoes and walk around in stocking feet for a minute or two. This gives your feet a taste of freedom and improves the blood flow.

Allow enough time for everyone to get moving before giving the next instructions.

Now move your toes left and right, up and down, stretching your feet in all directions.

Again, allow time for all to comply.

GUIDED STRETCH SCRIPT

Now that you've got the circulation going, it's time to give some attention to the muscles and tendons in your feet . . .
Sit down on the floor and begin slowly and gently rubbing these muscles and tendons . . .
working from the ankles toward the toes, massaging and loosening any tight places you find.

↪ *Pause 30 seconds.*

Be sure your other foot gets equal attention.

↪ *Pause 30 seconds.*

Now focus your attention on the soles of your feet . . .
Hold your foot with one hand . . .
and with the other, slap the sole of your foot in several places . . .
Run your fingers up and down the length of the sole . . .
very firmly, especially if you're ticklish . . .
to increase capillary width . . . and improve your blood flow.

↪ *Pause 15 seconds.*

Now hold your other foot with the opposite hand . . .
and slap this sole in several places . . .
This jarring of the sole's capillaries should help to avoid cramping.

↪ *Pause 15 seconds.*

Stop now and tune into your feet . . .
and the rest of your body . . . noticing any thoughts, feelings and sensations you are experiencing . . .

↪ *Pause 5 seconds.*

Bring these observations with you as you return your attention to the group.

GROUP PROCESSING OPTION

▨ Think of other nurturing touches or movements that your feet may appreciate at this moment. Give them what they need.

Sound

*Tune out stressful sounds. Tune in to silence
and the peaceful tunes of nature.*

GOAL

To learn how to shut out distracting noises.

TIME

8–10 minutes

SPECIAL CONSIDERATIONS

Ideal for stimulating discussion about stressful and pleasant sounds in
the workplace.

Find the quietest spot available for this imaging, away from office
noises or street sounds.

WARMUP

Although we usually think of our five senses as physical phenom-
ena, in fact, most of us have an incredible ability to create sensory
experiences using only our imagination and our memory of stored
sensory data.

We can conjure up a mental picture of a school classroom. We can
imagine the sensation of a tick crawling up our leg. We can recreate
the smell of popcorn or the taste of a fresh orange. We can hear the
intonation in people's voices long after they have spoken. In our
dreams, most of us are aware of conversations and other noises.

In this exercise, you will have the opportunity to fabricate
sound images.

GUIDED IMAGE SCRIPT

Be quiet now, and listen to the *silence* . . .

> *Pause 5 seconds.*

Hear your breath . . .
as you draw it in through your mouth or nose . . .
Hear it all the way down your trachea . . .
and into your lungs . . .

Listen to the gentle rhythm of your body . . .
relaxing as you request it to do so . . .

> *Pause 5 seconds.*

Now notice the sounds around you . . .

> *Pause 5 seconds.*

Isolate one sound . . . then let it fade . . .

> *Pause 5 seconds.*

Begin to listen to the silence between the sounds . . .

And as you mentally drift in thought . . . allow your body to relax.
Continue to relax . . . letting your eyes gently close . . .
Letting your relaxation continue to deepen.

As this relaxation continues . . . think about yourself sleeping in a
soft and comfortable bed in the nearest city . . .

> *Pause 5 seconds.*

Imagine that you have awakened in the early morning
from a deep sleep . . .
The city is as silent as falling snow . . .
It is about four o'clock in the morning . . .
and no light yet shines . . .
Perhaps you can hear the hum of the refrigerator in the
kitchen . . . but outside it is very still . . .

> *Pause 5 seconds.*

You lie quietly, half-awake, breathing easily, listening . . .
In the distance you hear the dull roar of a truck . . .

and the groaning motor gets louder as the truck approaches your street . . .

Gears grind as the vehicle slows to a halt . . . idling . . .
and you hear the thump of morning papers dropped off at a local vendor . . .

   ↶ *Pause 5 seconds.*

Now, the sky begins to brighten . . .
and the sounds of passing cars break the silence . . .
You listen for a moment when a car passes . . .
The tone of the motor drops slightly . . .
like that of a train whistle as the train whizzes by . . .

   ↶ *Pause 5 seconds.*

Occasionally a dog barks . . .
This is the time the milk truck drops off bottles of milk . . .
Imagine the truck slowing in front of your home and idling . . .
Soon you can hear the glass bottles clink when the milkman drops them gently on the front porch . . .

For a time the sound level remains low . . .
A few cars go by . . . and a front door slams . . .
The sky has brightened even more while people shower . . .
eat breakfast . . . and prepare for work . . .

Then you hear more doors slam . . .
wooden front doors . . . metal screen-doors . . .
car doors . . . even a sliding garage door . . .
Notice how many different sounds doors make in the morning . . .

   ↶ *Pause 5 seconds.*

Motors turn over, grumble, and roar . . . some catch and die . . .
others almost purr as they warm up . . .
Listen for each distinctive motor . . .
and try to picture the vehicle . . .

   ↶ *Pause 5 seconds.*

Among the other motors, you hear a heavy machine
that grumbles louder and more deeply than the others . . .

The gears grind painfully as it slows down near your window . . .
You know that sound . . . the school bus . . .
and you hear the running feet and boistrous shouts as kids run to
catch the bus . . .

⌒ *Pause 5 seconds.*

Now cars crowd the streets . . . horns honk, brakes screech . . .
The building crews arrive at a nearby construction site . . .
and soon you hear their machines start up . . .
Tractors growl . . . cranes roar . . .
and jackhammers pound the earth . . .
The city is now in full swing . . .
traffic is constant and heavy . . .

⌒ *Pause 5 seconds.*

Overhead you occasionally hear a jet or weather helicopter . . .
sometimes you notice the wail of a siren from a police car or an
ambulance . . .
motors race . . . irate drivers shout at one another . . .
a policeman blows his whistle . . .
Music blares from passing car radios and stereos carried by
kids . . .

⌒ *Pause 5 seconds.*

It is a solid barrage of noise . . .
hundreds of sounds . . .
and you decide to shut them down . . .

Focus your mind's eye on each source of sound . . .
and imagine it being taken far away . . . beyond hearing . . .

Turn each sound off . . .
by seeing it in your mind and then switching off its sound . . .
Radios . . . car engines . . . horns . . . the police whistle . . .
the siren . . . construction equipment . . .
airplanes . . . and shouting voices . . .

Gradually the tumultuous sounds fade in the distance.

⌒ *Pause 10 seconds.*

Once the noisy activity has ceased . . .
relax and notice the silence once again.

 Pause 5 seconds.

A much lighter, pleasantly-pitched tone reaches you . . .
and realizing it is a bird's song, you smile . . .

With this melodic sound filling your ears . . .
you are now ready to awaken . . .
and get out of bed to start your day . . .

 Pause 5 seconds.

In your mind, as you leave your bed . . .
you are also ready to awaken from this image
and continue with your day . . .

You are ready to awaken here and now . . .

Gently awaken . . . and open your eyes.

GROUP PROCESSING OPTION

 Recall any emotions you felt as you listened to the city come alive
and the sounds became more numerous. Think of three noises that
are daily distractions for you, and then imagine ways to shut them
off.

 Share your ideas with the group.

Bottle

Remember pleasant, soothing scents as an antidote to stress.

GOAL

To practice accessing olfactory memories.

TIME

8–10 minutes

MATERIALS

Small, covered bottle containing a substance with a pleasant, pungent odor, such as peppermint extract, orange slices, perfume, vanilla extract, lemon juice, herbs, or pine needles for each person.

SPECIAL CONSIDERATIONS

Best done with a small group since people need plenty of space to move around.

WARMUP

Many of us may think of imagery only as mental pictures. But we can also draw on our olfactory memories to recreate images of smells. This exercise will help you explore your ability to retain and recreate smells.

If you have difficulty bringing the smells to mind, try putting them in context—mentally find a vivid experience, positive or negative, which could be associated with each group of odors, then visualize the scene in detail. This should enable you to recreate the smell, or at least call to mind a sense of that smell.

GUIDED IMAGE SCRIPT

↪ *Give each person a "smell bottle" and ask participants to spread out along one side of the room.*

Pick up your bottle and open it . . .
don't hold it so close to your nostrils that the aroma is overpowering . . . just close enough for it to fill your senses . . .

Close your eyes and inhale the contents . . .
Allow yourself to sniff the aroma deeply . . .

↪ *Pause 10 seconds.*

Decide if this scent reminds you of any other odor . . .
perhaps it calls up pleasant memories of a particular person or occasion . . .

Take as much time as you need to experience the scent fully . . .

↪ *Pause 60 seconds.*

When you are through experiencing and analyzing . . .
put down the open bottle.
Open your eyes, stand up,
and move slowly toward the far end of the room . . .
trying to retain the smell as long as possible . . .

When the smell disappears . . .
note how far you are from the source.

If you reach the far wall and can still smell the aroma . . .
decide if it is drifting across the room . . .
or if you retain the smell in your memory.

Once you reach the far wall . . .
turn back and move slowly toward your bottle . . .
As you move, sniff the air constantly and deeply . . .
become aware of any changes in the quality and strength of the aroma . . .

Do you detect other aromas, memories, or ideas . . .
even fleetingly . . . as the scent grows powerful again?

Now that you are close to the bottle . . .
re-familiarize yourself with the aroma . . .

Sniff as fully and as deeply as you can . . .
for you are about to recreate it from memory . . .

When you feel you are ready . . . shut the bottle . . .
then swiftly go to a different part of the room
to see if you can still smell the bottle's aroma . . .

If you can . . . sniff for a minute or two . . .
and see if it diminishes over time . . . or if it is strengthened . . .

If you cannot smell the scent . . . return to the bottle and try again.

 ~ *Pause for several minutes while people practice
"remembering" their scents.*

Now that you have stretched your olfactory sense . . .
you can try working solely with your imagination.

Sit down and settle in once again . . .
Draw your attention back to your breathing . . .
and as you relax, close your eyes once again . . .

Call upon your powers of visualization, or any other sense,
to support you . . . as you try to recreate odors associated with
several different images.

First, imagine breathing in the fresh air of the country . . .
with all its pungent odors . . . wheat and grasses . . .
mint . . . horses . . . cows . . . sheep . . . pine trees.

 ~ *Pause 30 seconds.*

Now imagine inhaling smells of the polluted city . . .
dust . . . smoke . . . sulfur . . . exhaust fumes . . .
Make the image as vivid as possible in your mind and then pay
attention to the aromas.

 ~ *Pause 30 seconds.*

Now bring to your mind some more intimate smells . . .
incense . . . candles . . . scented soaps . . . baby powder . . .

 ~ *Pause 30 seconds.*

And now, recall one of your favorite foods . . .
you may even be able to taste this food . . .
Savor this sensation.

⤳ Pause 30 seconds.

Now that your senses are active and alert . . .
it is time for you to become active and alert as well . . .

Gently wiggle your toes and fingers . . .
notice the warmth or tingling as your body reawakens . . .
Stretch your arms and legs a bit, allowing your body and mind to
reawaken and focus on the present . . .

When you are ready . . .
open your eyes . . .
and come to full alertness . . .
feeling refreshed and revitalized.

GROUP PROCESSING OPTION

Find a partner and share the most vivid, pleasant memory that was
associated with specific odors. What other odors or memories did the
smell of the bottle scent trigger?

Attitude Change

Move from agitation or anger to self-control and
peace as you imagine all sides of an issue.

GOAL

To effect conscious attitude change.

TIME

4–5 minutes

SPECIAL CONSIDERATIONS

Ideal for use in worksite presentations on change and conflict resolution.

WARMUP

▧ A key component in life is one's attitude and ability to shift gears emotionally.

▧ Attitude is the result of a conscious, personal decision. No one or nothing else can determine your attitude. You are totally in control of this aspect of your experience.

▧ To take advantage of this autonomy, practice manipulating your attitudes and notice how your personal belief system relies on attitude.

GUIDED IMAGE SCRIPT

Slowly let your mind go blank . . .
until you come to a state of mental relaxation . . .

And as your mind becomes calm and quiet . . .
your body responds naturally, in turn . . .

Notice how your breathing may be slowing down as you relax . . .

Allow your eyes to close . . .
as you enjoy this deepening relaxation . . .

    ↶ *Pause 15 seconds.*

In the calm and quiet of your mind . . .
imagine a conference room . . .
with a table and two chairs across from each other.

Think about a pressing issue . . .
where you've already formed an opinion . . .
It could be any personal, social, or routine issue on which you have
already made a decision one way or another . . .

    ↶ *Pause 15 seconds.*

Once you have an issue in mind,
mentally take the opposite side of the issue . . .
that is, be your own opponent for a few minutes . . .
and argue the reverse of what you would normally contend . . .

    ↶ *Pause 30–40 seconds.*

After defending something contrary to your personal beliefs . . .
notice how your attitude might change . . .
from relatively calm to heated or disturbed . . .

    ↶ *Pause 5–10 seconds.*

Now, mentally defend the same side of the issue,
but this time adopt a positive attitude toward it . . .
defend it with a smile and a hope that something good will
result . . .

    ↶ *Pause 30–40 seconds.*

Notice that your attitude is under your control . . .
and that just by deciding to feel a certain way . . .
you can change your attitude.

    ↶ *Pause 5 seconds.*

Take another moment or two before coming back to the
present . . .

Bring back with you any thoughts you have about this
experience . . .

Note those actions and behaviors you would change . . .
and those you would continue in the future . . .

It is time to come back . . . to the here and now.
Open your eyes . . .
noticing how clear your mind is . . .

Your eyes are open now, and you have returned to the present.

GROUP PROCESSING OPTION

Select one issue that you have strong feelings about. Decide to change your attitude and practice this for one week.

Talk to a friend or co-worker about the results.

Chapter 6

SCRIPTS *for* CENTERING

The simple images in this chapter focus on the process of releasing tension or anxiety, and returning to a state of harmony and balance. Participants regain perspective through metaphors while they renew hope and faith that even in a changing world they can know their purpose and special place.

Blanketed in Relaxation

Peel away restrictive layers to emerge with freedom.

GOAL

To become relaxed and centered.

TIME

2–3 minutes

SPECIAL CONSIDERATIONS

This image is especially useful for quick relaxation—or as preparation for more complicated guided imagery. You may want to use this script at the beginning of each relaxation session as a transition exercise.

GUIDED IMAGE SCRIPT

Close your eyes now,
and as I count to *three,* take a slow, deep breath . . .
filling up your lungs fully . . .
One . . . two . . . three . . .
Hold your breath . . . and now exhale with a slight sigh . . .

As you continue to breathe slowly and deeply, imagine that you are lying on a small bed in a large, undecorated room . . .
You lie on your back, covered by several heavy blankets . . .
They stretch from under your chin . . .
down over your body . . . down to your toes
where they are all tucked under the corners of the mattress . . .

As you relax quietly under the blankets,
the top blanket magically peels its corners from under the mattress
and slowly begins to roll off your body . . .
The weight on your body lessens.

The next blanket does the same . . . and the next . . .

Your breathing becomes less labored . . .
The weight on your body slowly becomes less and less . . .

⁎ *Pause 5 seconds.*

The next blanket rolls off.
And the next . . . and the next . . .
You are now able to move your arms and legs freely.

⁎ *Pause 5 seconds.*

Now you have only one light blanket covering your body . . .
You feel almost no weight on your body . . .
but you discover that the last blanket is not moving by itself . . .

With your limbs' newfound freedom,
you discover that you can remove the blanket by yourself . . .
You take the blanket in your hands and peel it off your body,
dropping it on the floor atop the rest of the blankets.

You swing your legs off the bed . . .
letting your feet touch the warm floor . . .

You rise and walk away from the bed . . . and out of the room.

⁎ *Pause 10 seconds.*

Prepare yourself to return to us here in the room . . .
fully alert and refreshed . . .
When I count to three,
you will take a deep breath . . . hold it . . .
and breathe out with a slight sigh while gently opening your eyes.

Ready? . . . One . . . two . . . three . . .
Hold your breath . . . and now exhale with a slight sigh . . .

Open your eyes slowly and let in the sight of the room.

GROUP PROCESSING OPTION

As a group, discuss how this imaging experience relates to the
stress that blankets your life and how it restricts you.

Icicle

*Contemplate a simple change
in nature and find clarity.*

GOAL

To become centered.

TIME

2–3 minutes

SPECIAL CONSIDERATIONS

Especially helpful for groups working on coping with change and
learning to let go.

GUIDED IMAGE SCRIPT

Life is made up of many rhythmic patterns . . .

Begin by listening to the rhythm of your breathing . . .
as you take three deep breaths . . .
Gently and slowly breathe in and out . . .
in and out . . . in and out . . .

↶ *Pause 10 seconds.*

On your third exhalation, close your eyes . . .
and feel your body slowing down . . .
as you give in to the rhythm of your breathing . . .

Continue breathing deeply . . .
enjoying the feeling of increasing relaxation.

↶ *Pause 5 seconds.*

Listen, in your mind, to the sound of a faucet dripping . . .

Allow the dripping to slow down as you relax . . .
and when the dripping sound stops . . .
you drift into a deeper state of relaxation . . .

Imagine you are in a forest in winter . . .

⌐ Pause 5 seconds.

Picture a tree with one large icicle remaining . . .
hanging onto a branch . . .
frozen there throughout the long winter.

⌐ Pause 5 seconds.

At last . . . spring has arrived . . .
And with it comes warm air that will soften the icicle . . .

Watch the icicle begin to melt . . . as it gives way to the change of
seasons . . .
just as your tension melts away with the warmth of your breathing.

⌐ Pause 5 seconds.

Eventually the icicle melts enough to let go of the branch . . .
Watch as it falls softly into a remaining pile of snow.

As the icicle comes to its final resting place . . .
having released its tight grip . . .
so you have come to a resting place.

This is your cue to slowly open your eyes . . .

Take your time as you return to the present . . .

Like the melting icicle . . . you also have let go . . .
and relaxed for this time.

You can now open your eyes and go on with your day . . .
relaxed and transformed.

GROUP PROCESSING OPTION

▨ What changes in your outlook did you notice as you watched the
icicle melt and fall to the ground?

▨ Share your insights with your group.

Excess Baggage

Escape mental and physical burdens in this transformation to relaxation.

GOAL

Physical and mental relaxation.

TIME

5–8 minutes

GUIDED IMAGE SCRIPT

Make yourself comfortable . . .
Unbuckle your belt if it constricts your breathing . . .
and close your eyes . . .

Focus on your breathing . . .
breathing with your belly . . .
Imagine breathing in calm energy,
however you imagine that to be . . .
and breathing out negative energy . . .
as you breathe deeply in and out . . .

🖙 *Pause 10 seconds.*

In your mind, imagine that you enter a room carrying baggage . . .
You have bags slung on each shoulder, briefcases in each hand . . .
your clothes are heavy . . .
Your muscles ache.

You set all the baggage down . . . and lie flat on the firm floor.

The ceiling above gives way to a bright blue sky . . .
and suddenly all around you are the sounds of crashing waves . . .
You can almost smell the sea salt.

The sun is low . . .
the light is now turning orange, pink, purple . . .
and now dark, dark, blue . . .

Pause 5 seconds.

As you lie flat, you bend and rotate your legs . . .
stretching your muscles . . .
They are thirsty for oxygen, and soon they have it.

Pause 10 seconds.

Allow your arms and back to stretch long like a rubber band . . .
reaching, arching upward . . .
then ease them slowly back into place . . .
They are breathing now, too.

Pause 10 seconds.

Soon every muscle in your body will receive fresh oxygen from the
ocean air . . . taken in by your lungs . . .
You will be relaxed in body . . .
and prepared to relax in mind . . .

Pause 10 seconds.

You are now refreshed as you prepare to come back to the room . . .
You have been released from your heavy burdens . . .

Open your eyes . . .
wiggle your feet and toes . . .
stretch your arms . . . hands . . . and fingers . . .

Stretch your entire body if you need to at this time
and feel the gentle relaxation flowing through you.

GROUP PROCESSING OPTION

Share with others in your small group what might have been in
your baggage at the beginning of this image, and what insight you
gained from the visualization.

Balloon

*Let go of your tension as you
release the air in an imaginary balloon.*

GOAL

To relax and reduce tension.

TIME

2–3 minutes

MATERIALS

Balloons for all participants, if Group Processing Option is used.

SPECIAL CONSIDERATIONS

Appropriate for work groups or classes focused on relaxation or stress management.

GUIDED IMAGE SCRIPT

Make yourself comfortable in your chair . . .
Adjust your body . . . slide around . . . until you feel the small of
your back being cradled by the chair that supports you . . .
Your shoulders are relaxed and free, loose, not tight . . .

Think about yourself floating like a cloud . . .
you are as light as a feather . . .

    ↬ *Pause 5 seconds.*

Feel yourself soar freely like a bird . . .
high in the air . . .

    ↬ *Pause 5 seconds.*

Or feel like a leaf . . .
being gently carried by the currents of the wind.

    ↬ *Pause 5 seconds.*

As you focus on these thoughts and feelings,
you become more relaxed . . .

To deepen this experience . . .
allow yourself to relax fully . . .
as I count backwards from ten to one . . .
With each descending number, you will be more relaxed.

By the time I reach the number five . . .
your eyes will close . . .
and by the time I reach the number one . . .
you will be in a deeper state of relaxation than you are now.

Make sure to read the numbers slowly and evenly as participants relax. It helps to take a deep breath yourself between each number.

Ten . . . nine . . . eight . . . seven . . . six . . .

five . . . your eyes are closed . . .

four . . . you are more relaxed . . .

three . . . you are drifting into a profound state of relaxation . . .

two . . . you are calm and relaxed . . .

and one . . . fully relaxed.

Begin to think about round objects . . .
balls of all different sizes . . .

Pause 10 seconds.

Now imagine one particular ball . . .
Picture it in the form of a blown-up balloon.
Allow the image of this balloon to form clearly . . .
Imagine it has been blown up to its maximum capacity.

Once you have the balloon clear in your mind . . .
imagine how this balloon feels . . .
full . . . tense . . . and distended . . .

Hold that thought for a moment . . .

Pause 15 seconds.

Now imagine letting go . . .
deflating the balloon . . .
releasing all the trapped air . . .

Experience the sensation of the air as it lets go . . .
whooshing eagerly out leaving the balloon empty . . .
relaxed . . . and back in its natural form.

As the balloon returns to its original shape . . .
it is time for you, too, to return to your surroundings . . .

As you come back . . .
bring back with you any sensations or thoughts from this experience
that you wish.

Feel now the chair cradling your back . . .
and tune into my voice . . .
as you open your eyes and return to the room.

GROUP PROCESSING OPTION

 Give each person a balloon and give instructions.

▓ Blow up the balloon as full as possible without breaking it. Imagine blowing all your tension into the balloon.

Hold the balloon between your fingers while you imagine all the tension inside. When told to let go, release the balloon.

▓ Now let go and release the balloon. Then discuss with a neighbor how it felt to let go of your tension.

Martial Arts Stretch

*Relax and tune in to your center
using upper body stretches adapted from the martial arts.*

GOAL

To relax and get centered.

TIME

6–8 minutes

SPECIAL CONSIDERATIONS

Best when participants are wearing loose, comfortable clothing.

Stretching should be done on mats or a comfortable, carpeted floor.

*↬ You may want to prepare a handout listing books on
stretching to give participants. A complete guide for
stretching your muscles may be found at many health food
stores, bookstores, and local fitness centers.*

WARMUP

▨ Certain martial artists advise that all relaxation take place seated in
a position called *sowatei*, pronounced "so-whah-tay."

To accomplish this, tuck your legs underneath so you are sitting on
your feet, with your hands on your knees.

▨ From here, stretches of the neck, arms, wrists, and back are
completed by gently and steadily rolling the corresponding part of the
body.

When you stretch your head and arms, or any other routine you have
adopted, remember to stretch slowly and completely, never bouncing
or over-extending.

*↬ Encourage people to trust their instincts as to what
parts of their body they want to stretch during the last part
of the exercise.*

GUIDED STRETCH SCRIPT

Close your eyes . . . and breathe slowly and deeply . . .
in through the nose and out through the mouth . . .

Do this for about a minute . . .

 ↜ Pause 45–60 seconds.

Now rotate your head counterclockwise . . . then clockwise . . .
slowly and gently . . . ten rotations in each direction . . .

 *↜ Pause. Watch the group to determine when most
 people have made ten rotations.*

Now rotate your arms forward . . . then backward . . .
slowly . . . ten rotations in each direction . . .

 ↜ Pause until most people have made the ten rotations.

Again, rotate your head counterclockwise . . . then clockwise . . .
slowly and gently . . . ten rotations in each direction . . .

 ↜ Pause until most people are finished.

And again, rotate your arms forward . . . then backward . . .
slowly . . . ten rotations in each direction . . .

 ↜ Pause until most people are ready to move on.

Now shake your wrists out . . .
and open your eyes . . .

Continue stretching any other parts of your body that feel tight or
tense.

GROUP PROCESSING OPTION

▩ Share with the group other stretching exercises that you have
found helpful.

Thunderstorm

*Focus on feelings of peace and new life
in the aftermath of a thunderstorm.*

GOAL
To become centered and relaxed.

TIME
3–4 minutes

SPECIAL CONSIDERATIONS
Because the Group Processing Option invites more personal sharing,
it should be done only if there is a high degree of trust in the group,
and if greater intimacy is an appropriate goal for the audience and
setting.

GUIDED IMAGE SCRIPT

It's time now to be quiet . . . time to be centered.
Tune out the noises and distractions of the day . . .
and tune in to your heartbeat . . .
tune in to your pulse.

Everything is quiet, except for the sound of your body . . .

You breathe deeply in and out . . .
and your heart pounds gently, yet solidly in your chest.
Feel the sound of your heart beating . . .
and allow it to carry you in a steady, measured,
rhythmic motion . . .

Hear your breath whoosh in and out . . .
in and out . . .
Tune in to the rhythm of life as you close your eyes.

    Pause 10 seconds.

Your heartbeat is steady . . . like the sound of a clock ticking . . .
Your breathing is regular and deep . . .
and your eyes are closed.
The rhythm of your body carries you further and further into a state
of deep relaxation . . .

Imagine yourself carried into a meadow . . .
with mountains all around you . . .

See yourself lying on your back in a protective cocoon . . .
allowing your mind to wander . . . watching the clouds . . .

⤺ *Pause 10 seconds.*

As you drift in thought . . .
imagine that a thunderstorm is approaching . . .

You are safe in your cocoon as the clouds darken . . .
and warm rain begins to pour . . .
but you can hear the clashing sounds of the storm . . .
and sense its enormous energy . . .
as bright flashes of lightning are quickly followed by a loud crack of
thunder . . .

⤺ *Pause 10 seconds.*

Gradually . . . the rain lessens . . .
and you notice the growing space between the lightning and the
thunder.

As the storm moves further away . . .
you hear less and less noise . . .
It grows progressively quieter . . .
as the storm moves into the distance . . .

Feel yourself letting go as the storm passes . . .
Let the quiet help carry you into an open . . .
calm . . . state of repose.

As you drift into a state of relaxation . . .
notice the freshness of the wet green grass and leafy trees.

Having bathed in this experience, it is time now to awaken . . .

You will awaken . . . and open your eyes . . . now . . .
feeling relaxed and refreshed from your thunderstorm.

GROUP PROCESSING OPTION

▨ Recall a time when you experienced a storm in your personal life. What were some of the ways you stayed centered?

▨ Share your recollections with the group.

↪ *Be sure to keep the discussion focused on the process of how people stayed centered, rather than the content of their stories. Identify common themes for the group.*

Change of Seasons

*Experience a strong sense of cosmic belonging
and harmony with nature as you visualize
seasonal changes in the landscape.*

GOAL

To become centered and relaxed.

To stimulate feelings of flexibility, maturity, and renewal.

TIME

8–10 minutes

MATERIALS

A poster or postcard of a farm scene (optional).

SPECIAL CONSIDERATIONS

Especially appropriate for work groups who are involved with
seasonal changes at the worksite. Ideal for planning and goal-setting,
and for staff retreats.

Can be done outdoors, if weather and group size permit.

WARMUP

As seasons give way to one another, they affect the rhythm of our
daily lives and moods. They slow us down or pick us up, often
without our noticing it.

In this exercise you will experience a number of seasonal cycles.

GUIDED IMAGE SCRIPT

It's time to change the rhythm of your life for a bit . . .

Take a moment to get settled and relaxed . . .
and then begin to tune in to the rhythm of your breathing . . .
Notice the flow of air as you slowly breathe out and in . . .
exhaling and inhaling in a relaxed, steady rhythm.

    ✑ *Pause 5 seconds.*

As you continue to breathe slowly and rhythmically . . .
close your eyes . . .
and bring to your mind a mental image of a farm scene . . .
It may be one you have visited, seen, or read about . . .

    ✑ *Pause 5 seconds.*

Adjust your mental perspective as needed
so you can view the entire scene from a distance . . .
perhaps from a hillside overlooking the farm . . .
or through the window of a nice, warm house across the road . . .

As the images become clearer in your mind . . .
continue to relax comfortably and breathe easily . . .
while you concentrate on the farm scene.

    ✑ *Pause 5 seconds.*

First, you will observe animal activity through the seasons . . .

It is summer . . .
and animals are grazing . . .
cows' tails bat at buzzing flies . . .
sheep are sheared and lie about . . .
bees are visiting flowers for nectar . . .
fish loll at the surface of the pond.

    ✑ *Pause 15 seconds.*

It is fall . . .
the animals prepare for the cold weather . . .
horses and cows gather into groups . . .
birds take flight for warmer climates . . .
squirrels scamper to stockpile nuts . . .
frogs head for the bottom of the pond . . .

some animals grow heavier coats of fur or feathers . . .
long lines of geese fly south in the dark sky.

   ⌐ Pause 15 seconds.

It is winter . . .
animals are shut away in barns, lairs, and burrows . . .
many of them are sleeping . . .
a winter bird pecks about for seeds . . .
ducks waddle across the icy pond to a tiny black patch of water . . .
a horse shivers in the wind and shakes its head.

   ⌐ Pause 15 seconds.

It is spring . . .
animals are up and around . . .
chicks are hatching and chirping . . .
lambs, calves, and colts are born and totter on unsteady legs . . .
the air is alive with bees on the hunt for flowers . . .
the bigger animals gallop out to distant pastures with green grasses.

   ⌐ Pause 15 seconds.

Next, focus on human activities throughout the farming year . . .

It is summer . . .
you rise early in bright sunlight to feed the pigs and cows . . .
storm windows and heavy drapes are removed . . .
screen windows are opened and soft curtains rustle . . .
there is swimming, boating and fishing in the pond . . .
children play hide-and-seek in the cornfields . . .
crops are reaped and harvested, hay is baled . . .
it is warm . . .
and people fan themselves on the porch . . .
napping under shady oak trees.

   ⌐ Pause 15 seconds.

It is fall . . .
you are still rising early to feed the animals . . .
but it's darker out . . .
you're getting animals and buildings ready for cold weather . . .
cleaning windows, drapes, and curtains . . .
chopping and piling wood . . .

raking leaves . . .
picking and storing vegetables . . .
canning, preserving, baking freshly picked apples into pies . . .
making taffy apples and applesauce . . .
dancing at the grange hall in the evening.

↶ *Pause 15 seconds.*

It is winter . . .
and you awaken in darkness to feed animals . . .
you're tapping trees for maple syrup . . .
splitting firewood . . .
skating on the pond . . .
drawing the drapes and curtains . . .
stoking a roaring fire . . .
knitting, listening to music, repairing furniture, and reading.

↶ *Pause 15 seconds.*

It is spring . . .
windows are opened to catch fresh spring breezes . . .
and curtains are parted to welcome the sun . . .
you are turning up rich soil,
tilling the earth to plant new trees and vegetables . . .
helping to birth new animals . . .
digging trenches with a hoe . . .
dropping seeds for corn, beans, lettuce, radishes . . .
flying kites and picnicking.

↶ *Pause 15 seconds.*

Now you watch the changes in nature . . .

It is summer . . .
with bright sun . . .
long, hot days . . .
heavy, moist air . . .
afternoon thunderstorms . . .
green and yellow hills . . .
blossoms giving way to fruit . . .
wild thyme . . .
intense sunsets and sunrises.

↶ *Pause 15 seconds.*

It is fall . . .
when greens and yellows become
reds, oranges, purples . . .
leaves fall in heaps and blankets . . .
crackling, crisp leaves crunch underfoot . . .
smoke tinges the air . . .
pumpkins are harvested and carved . . .
fog drifts in the morning . . .
dark clouds gather in the sky . . .
stars twinkle and a yellow moon sits on the horizon.

    Pause 15 seconds.

It is winter . . .
with silence . . .
dark, cold, pristine whiteness . . .
then rushing, biting winds, and snow flurries . . .
stark, bare trees . . . snow-covered branches . . .
firm earth . . . tall evergreens . . .
short days and long nights.

    Pause 15 seconds.

It is spring . . .
a time for warm rains . . .
soft earth . . .
deep breaths of fresh air . . .
when plants spring to life . . .
vivid flowers bloom . . . trees fill with green leaves . . .
equal day and night . . .
rebirth . . .
rejuvenation . . .

    Pause 15 seconds.

Pause for a moment now,
no longer swept by these changing scenes . . .

Take a few more moments before opening your eyes
and returning from the farm scene to the present . . .

    Pause 5 seconds.

Begin to return . . .
Take a deep breath . . .
and while exhaling . . . open your eyes . . .
and return once again to your familiar surroundings.

GROUP PROCESSING OPTION

▦ Make a few quick notes about feelings you associated with each of the four seasons. Which seasons did you like the best and why? Which seasons did you like the least and why? How did all these changes make you feel? Did they seem too fast?

▦ Share your experience with a partner (or small group).

Chapter 7

SCRIPTS *for* CREATIVITY

The playful images in this chapter offer opportunities to renew, release, and transform creative energies. Participants soar above limitations, break out of old patterns, and make bold changes as they unleash their creative potential.

Eagle in the Sky

*Discover the freedom and weightlessness
of soaring like an imaginary eagle.*

GOAL

To enhance relaxation and creativity.

TIME

2–3 minutes

SPECIAL CONSIDERATIONS

Ideal for groups exploring creativity and relaxation as tools for
wellness and stress management.

If the Group Processing Option is used, participants will need
writing materials and an introduction to the use of dialogue in
journaling. Encourage playfulness and nonjudgmental expression
when writing.

GUIDED IMAGE SCRIPT

As you relax now and listen to my voice, think about yourself
melting into the most comfortable chair you own . . .

Pause 5 seconds.

As your body lets go and goes limp,
allow the feeling of weightlessness to take over . . .

Close your eyes . . .
and feel yourself floating . . . weightless and free . . .

Pause 10 seconds.

Imagine yourself resting outside . . .
under a clear blue sky . . .
and as you look up . . . you see a bald eagle.

Seemingly motionless and buoyant . . .
the eagle floats along the gentle currents of the wind . . .
moving effortlessly forward . . .

⤳ Pause 5 seconds.

As it moves . . .
you move in harmony with the bird
towards a state of serene relaxation . . .

Imagine yourself rising . . .
and soaring away from your tension and frustration . . .
motionless and buoyant on your own currents of relaxation.

⤳ Pause 15 seconds.

As the eagle slowly glides and drifts toward the horizon . . .
feel yourself re-emerging from this exercise . . .

Become more aware of your body . . .
become more aware of the room . . .
and finally, open your eyes and awaken.

GROUP PROCESSING OPTION

▨ Write a short dialogue with the eagle. Let your thoughts and
feelings emerge freely without censorship or judgment. Write for
three to five minutes.

*⤳ When the group starts getting restless, announce one
minute to finish. Then ask for volunteers to read their
dialogues out loud. Instruct the rest of the group to listen
respectfully but not comment on the writings of others.
Allow time for all who want to read to do so.*

Leg Stretch

*Release tension and free up new energy
with an easy sensory stretch routine.*

GOAL

To relax and revitalize.

TIME

4–5 minutes

SPECIAL CONSIDERATIONS

Excellent process for worksite wellness programs.

This exercise requires a large, open space for stretching. Participants should be wearing loose, comfortable clothing.

WARMUP

▮ Have participants find an open place on the floor as you caution them to avoid stretching on a bed or couch.

GUIDED STRETCH SCRIPT

Sit down on the floor . . . with your back straight and your legs stretched out straight in front of your body.

As you get comfortable, place your knees together . . .
raise your toes upward . . .
and lean down to touch your toes . . .

The objective is not to stretch your back . . .
Instead you will stretch and relax your hamstring and calf muscles . . .

Concentrate on these muscles while you stretch . . .
Remember to keep breathing . . .
As you hold the stretch for thirty seconds . . .

   ↬ *Pause 20 seconds.*

The next stretching technique concentrates on the front of your legs . . . the thigh muscles, called the *quadriceps* . . .

Sit on the floor with your legs directly out in front of you . . .
Place your left hand, palm down, on the floor
beside your left thigh . . .
Then, bend your right leg at the knee . . .
and with your right hand grasp your right ankle . . .
Pull your right foot under your right buttock . . .
so that you are sitting on your right foot . . .
Now lean back a few inches . . .
With this you should feel your right thigh being stretched . . .

Hold this for thirty seconds . . .

　↤ *Pause 20 seconds.*

Now, the other leg . . .

　↤ *Pause 30 seconds.*

This stretch should help decrease lactic acid in one of your body's largest muscle groups . . .
as well as making it easier for you to relax.

　↤ *Pause 5 seconds.*

When you have completed your stretches,
take note of any thoughts, feelings and sensations you are experiencing . . .

　↤ *Pause 5 seconds.*

When you have noted these,
you have completed this exercise for now.

GROUP PROCESSING OPTION

▨ Share with the group several simple leg stretches that could be done throughout the day, at work or home.

HOMEWORK

▨ Experiment in the coming week with using these stretches.

Heat

*Renew your spirit as you imagine
burning firewood transforming matter to energy.*

GOAL

To let go of tension.

To generate new energy for creativity.

TIME

2–3 minutes

SPECIAL CONSIDERATIONS

A quick energizer for any task-focused group at work or in the community.

Make sure the physical environment is a moderately warm, comfortable temperature for people—imagining a glowing fire in a chilly room is tough.

WARMUP

The natural world constantly strives for a state of balance. All actions are counterbalanced by reactions, as matter is transformed into energy.

When wood burns, the wood changes form. Its counterbalance is heat.

GUIDED IMAGE SCRIPT

Begin by concentrating on your breathing . . .
As you inhale, feel your body expand . . .
As you exhale, feel your body let go . . .

⤻ *Pause 10 seconds.*

Continue to inhale and exhale easily . . .
Now, as you close your eyes,
your breath appears as a visible gas . . .
As you exhale, imagine watching your breath as it leaves your lips
in a cloud of white or blue or orange mist . . .

 Pause 5 seconds.

As you continue to relax . . .
imagine yourself as a piece of wood
blazing on a campfire or in a fireplace . . .

 Pause 5 seconds.

As the fire burns, picture yourself being transformed from a solid
state of matter . . . into radiant energy and warmth . . .

As the fire in your mental image continues to transform the solid
wood to radiant energy . . .
allow all the tension in your body to be released
in the same, natural way . . .
freeing knots of stress and tension . . .
transforming any tightness into flowing energy
that radiates freely through your body . . .
warming and soothing . . .

 Pause 20 seconds.

As the smoke begins to clear from the warm, burning firewood,
it is time to return . . .

Become aware of your breathing . . .
and slowly come to a conscious state of mind.

As you breathe in . . . and out . . .
in . . . and out . . . in . . . and out . . .

 Pause 5 seconds.

It's now time to open your eyes and return . . .
bringing the glow of the fire
and your renewed energy to the rest of your day.

GROUP PROCESSING OPTION

▇ Think silently of one quick thing you could do in the present which could rekindle your energy. Without revealing your intentions, take the next two or three minutes to rekindle your energy using this strategy.

⌒ Reconvene the group and talk about what people did and how it worked.

Walk through the Forest

*Explore the limitless potential of your imagination when
you enter an enchanted house in the forest.*

GOAL

To enhance creativity by realizing the power of the mind.

TIME

8 minutes

GUIDED IMAGE SCRIPT

Focus on your breathing . . . breathing with your belly . . .
Let your breath find its own most comfortable rhythm.

∾ *Pause 10 seconds.*

Imagine breathing in calming energy as you inhale . . .
and imagine releasing tensions as you exhale . . .
Breathe this way for three very slow and deep breaths . . .
inhale calming energy . . . and exhale tensions . . .
closing your eyes as you breathe deeply.

∾ *Pause 15 seconds.*

Become more and more present in this place . . .
in this moment . . . with each breath you inhale and exhale.

Your thoughts move in and out of your awareness
as easily as you breathe in and out . . .
no resistance . . . no attachment . . .

∾ *Pause 5 seconds.*

Here, thoughts, feelings, and sensations
move through your awareness as easily as
the breath you exhale through your nose or mouth . . .

Imagine for a moment that you are walking through a forest . . .
a forest dense with trees and undergrowth . . .
so dense that branches and tree trunks seem sewn together . . .
nearly blocking your path . . .
The sun shines overhead, but you cannot feel its warmth . . .
The shadows of birds dance around, but you cannot see their flight.
You hear nothing.

> *Pause 5 seconds.*

Suddenly the trees give way to a massive clearing . . .
in which stands a magnificent enchanted house.
A giant key lies on the welcome mat . . .

> *Pause 5 seconds.*

You unlock the door . . .
and as you enter the house, your senses spring to life . . .

A rush of cool air hits your skin . . .
and the sounds of the birds outside echo within the walls.

Inside you see hundreds of archways . . .
opening onto wide, lighted halls, with no visible end . . .
leading to mazes of intriguing rooms . . .

> *Pause 5 seconds.*

You travel from room to room, exploring . . .
experiencing all of what each room has to offer . . .
allowing each new room to come alive in you mind
as you step across the threshold . . .

You may find long stretches of valley landscape . . .
blue seas with uninterrupted horizons . . .
wide expanses of people, places, and events
in which to immerse yourself . . .
a carnival . . . a woodworking shop . . . a wedding . . .
a tropical island . . . a spaceship . . . a baseball game . . .

Allow your mind to roam freely from room to room . . .
immersing yourself in whatever places or events or people
you discover on your tour of the enchanted house . . .

> *Pause for several minutes of exploration.*

Now, through one archway you see the forest where you were walking . . . and realizing that these images were all in your mind to begin with . . . you step back inside the forest.

Its paths are now wide and cleared of overgrowth,
and your walk through it is uninterrupted, relaxing, and healing.
Your forest walk has shown you the limitless potential of your mind.
Whatever you can imagine, can happen.

The very fact that you can imagine a vision makes it possible . . .
makes it probable . . . makes it real . . .
Tell yourself this now.

      Pause 5 seconds.

If you ever need to reinforce this energy,
all you need to do is momentarily remember this forest walk.

When you're ready to come back to the room,
you can open your eyes . . .
knowing that this energy continues to move through you.

GROUP PROCESSING OPTION

Reflect on one of the challenges you are facing in your life right now. Then quickly sketch one of the rooms you visited in your enchanted house, and jot down some notes about how the perspective or content of this room's landscape could apply to solving your problem or meeting your challenge.

Share your drawing and conclusions with others in your small group (or a partner).

Design a Glass

Unleash your creative imagination
as you explore shape, color, words, texture, and taste.

GOAL

To enhance creativity through sensory images.

TIME

6–8 minutes

MATERIALS

Clear, ordinary drinking glass for each participant.

SPECIAL CONSIDERATIONS

Appropriate for any group exploring the role of creativity in problem-solving and self-fulfillment.

WARMUP

In this exercise, you will explore your ability to visualize, using a drinking glass to start the creative process.

There is no right or wrong way to create images. For example, the ability to visualize specific colors is not necessarily superior to the ability to perceive differences.

Whatever comes to mind during imagery is instructive and useful.

Remember, you can always adjust whatever you imagine, recreating the image until it is just right for now.

Give each participant a clear drinking glass before starting the visualization.

Guided Image Script

Inhale and exhale slowly and completely three times . . .

One . . .

    Pause 5 seconds.

Two . . .

    Pause 5 seconds.

Three . . .

    Pause 5 seconds.

Continue this easy, relaxed breathing
as you embark on this exercise in creativity . . .
You are going to design a drinking glass . . .

Pick up your drinking glass . . . and examine it closely . . .
Notice how solid and clear it is . . .

Study the glass until you have its shape and mass
clearly in your mind . . .
Notice how it catches the light,
especially inside the gently curved bottom . . .
Concentrate on the glass . . .

Now close your eyes . . .
and recall the image of the glass.

    Pause 5 seconds.

Now that the glass is in your mind,
you are going to mold it
as if it were soft, clear clay . . .

You can stretch it vertically . . . or horizontally . . .
add decorations . . . or a wider base . . .
or a squeezed middle . . . or a fancy handle . . .
or whatever you wish . . .

Move deliberately and carefully . . .
impose each adjustment slowly . . .
and after each change . . . re-examine the glass.
If you don't like the result, try something else . . .

DESIGN A GLASS

⤺ Pause 30 seconds.

Once you have designed the shape of your glass . . .
you are ready to engrave something on its inner surface . . .
The message should appear rough and cloudy . . .
whiter than the rest of the glass . . .
You could etch your name . . . or someone else's . . .
or a short message . . . such as coffee . . . or tea . . .
or any message or design you choose . . .

After the glass has been engraved . . .
study it until you feel that it is permanent.

⤺ Pause 20 seconds.

Now fill your glass with a liquid . . .
and notice how that liquid colors the glass . . .
If your glass is thicker in certain places than in others . . .
notice how that affects the apparent color of the liquid.

⤺ Pause 20 seconds.

Now put a clear straw into the glass of liquid . . .

Once the straw has settled, change its appearance . . .
give it a solid color . . . or two . . .
make it candy-striped or polka-dotted . . .
you might change its length and shape . . .

⤺ Pause 15 seconds.

Again, make sure that once you have chosen a design
for your straw . . .
you study it long enough to give it permanence.

⤺ Pause 10 seconds.

Finally . . . if you choose . . .
you may drink the liquid . . .
Remember that you can adjust its taste and temperature . . .
you may decide to have it hot or cold . . .
sweet or bitter . . . tangy . . . carbonated . . .
or anything else.

⤺ Pause 10 seconds.

Think now about how satisfying . . .
and thirst-quenching the liquid is . . .

And as you think about the liquid,
you have completed the last step . . .
It is now time for you to awaken . . .
and open your eyes . . .

Feel how refreshed your body is at this time . . .
how relaxed . . . how peaceful you feel . . .

Prepare yourself to return to the room on the count of three . . .

One . . .

Two . . .

Three.

GROUP PROCESSING OPTION

■ Share your glass design visualization experience with a partner.

Did you immediately choose the design, or experiment with a number of different adjustments? What factors influenced your decisions?

Describe your experience and reflect on how it felt to be creative.

Poll the group on how the need for creativity is nourished for each individual.

Picture

Step into a relaxing scene and use it to create an imaginary ideal environment.

GOAL

To stimulate creativity.

TIME

6–8 minutes

MATERIALS

Photograph of a relaxing scene (without people in it) for each participant.

SPECIAL CONSIDERATIONS

Especially appropriate for groups where personal empowerment and effecting change is a desired goal.

Participants need to prepare for this exercise by searching (at home) for a photograph that depicts a simple, uncluttered, relaxing scene—perhaps a stream, a country road, a single tree, or a farm pasture.

If necessary, the trainer could provide appropriate postcards, posters or photos.

WARMUP

▨ In this era of instant news photography and glossy fashion and nature magazines, we are bombarded with images of places and events that are out of reach: vacation spots we wish we could visit, sports triumphs we wish we could have witnessed or experienced firsthand, funny scenes, or great historical moments.

▨ In this exercise you will use a picture of a scene that is finite in time and space. You will put yourself into this scene, and expand its frontiers as you wish.

■ The more times you do this exercise, the more proficient you will become at breaking out of patterns and limitations in your creativity.

■ You will learn that things do not have to be as they *are*. At any moment you can make them simpler or more complex than they might appear.

GUIDED IMAGE SCRIPT

Settle yourself comfortably
and turn your attention to your breathing . . .
breathing in and out deeply, slowly and naturally . . .

Pause 5 seconds.

As you continue to breathe deeply and naturally . . .
feel all your tension dissolving and draining away . . .

Pause 15 seconds.

With the next breath . . . pick up your picture . . .
and continue to breathe deeply
as you study the scene in your picture carefully . . .
Study it long enough so that you can see it with your eyes closed . . .

Pause 10 seconds.

Now . . . as you close your eyes and continue to relax . . .
move closer to the scene in the picture . . .
The deeper your relaxation . . .
the further you move into the scene . . .

When you are fully relaxed . . .
allow yourself to step into the scene entirely . . .

Pause 10 seconds.

Now that you are standing inside the scene in the picture . . .
take careful note of everything around you . . .
allow yourself to be aware of and examine everything in the setting.

Pause 5 seconds.

Notice all that is apparent to your five senses . . .

What are the sights . . . sounds . . . smells . . . tastes . . .
and textures you are experiencing?

⤳ *Pause 10 seconds.*

Do you notice any movement . . .
or is everything still? . . .

How does this place make you feel?

⤳ *Pause 10 seconds.*

Once you have taken full account of the immediate area . . .
look around . . . and choose a direction in which you would like to
walk . . .

When you feel ready, start walking in that direction . . .

⤳ *Pause 5 seconds.*

As you walk, pay close attention to anything that changes . . .
certain aspects of your surroundings will be altered . . .
some may be left behind . . .

Remember that you can change anything you see or encounter . . .
wherever you walk, whatever you see . . .
you have the power to adjust, transform, or remove it . . .

You have control over the course of your stroll.

⤳ *Pause 5 seconds.*

Continuing on your way . . .
take note of the things that are familiar . . .
and the things you do not recognize . . .

If you wish to pause and examine any of them more closely, do so.

⤳ *Pause 10 seconds.*

Now that you have explored the world inside
and beyond the original picture . . .
it is time to go back . . .

You are in no hurry . . .
but you retrace your steps . . .
noticing in reverse all the things you have passed . . .

They are all familiar to you now . . .
and you remind yourself that you put them there . . .

⌣ Pause 10 seconds.

Eventually you arrive back at the original scene of the picture . . .
and place yourself where you can see the whole scene . . .
as it was when you first arrived.

As you stand in that original spot . . .
allow your consciousness to slowly return . . .

⌣ Pause 5 seconds.

You are waking up . . .
and feeling yourself coming out of the picture . . .

The more you awaken . . .
the further you move from the picture's scene . . .

Feel your mind become calm and quiet . . .
Feel your mind become clear and spacious . . .
as spacious as the wide-open sky . . .

Allow yourself to take a deep breath . . .
and as you exhale, slowly open your eyes . . .

Before you is the picture you just visited . . .
you are awake.

GROUP PROCESSING OPTION

Find a partner and share your visual journey.

Did you change anything in your surroundings? Tell what you changed and how it felt to do this.

How did your feelings about the original picture you chose change after the exercise, if at all? Did you feel any desire to begin again, perhaps to walk in a different direction?

Fantasy

Explore subconscious fantasies and the potential consequences of living them out.

GOAL

To promote self-awareness and creativity.

TIME

8–10 minutes

SPECIAL CONSIDERATIONS

Most appropriate for therapy/growth groups where the leader has been able to assess risk for participants involved in fantasy.

Could be used in training groups for helping professionals.

⌐ Because this may be a scary exercise for some people, an introductory chalktalk on fantasy is important. Be sure to process the guided image afterwards, so participants feel safe and confident regarding destructive fantasies. Be alert to possible shame responses from negative fantasies.

WARMUP

▨ Everyone has fantasies. A fantasy takes us away from our present situation and allows us to visit a place or to have an experience that takes place solely in our mind.

Fantasies can range from positive, pure and noble—like being responsible for world peace activities—to those which might be deemed negative and evil by most standards, or at best nonproductive.

▨ All fantasies flow from a source within us, and therefore have important reasons for existence.

Some people may be uncomfortable with their fantasies, reluctant to discuss them with others, or even unwilling to admit that they fantasize. They may feel that the acknowledgment of a certain fantasy might be too scary or threatening to their daily existence.

If a fantasy involves performance of a tremendous good, identifying it can enable you to enact some small part of it with your limited resources.

A fantasy may involve evil or monumental waste; in that case, if you acknowledge it, you can begin to shape it, tame it and put it in perspective.

An unacknowledged fantasy, though it appears harmlessly buried, still works its power on your life through subconscious desires. Therefore, it is much healthier to open the door and face it.

In this experience you are going to allow yourself to live out a fantasy of your choice, within the safety and confines of your imagination. It may be something incredibly good that you never had the power to do, or it may be something you could never allow yourself to act out.

Whatever you experience, you must remember that it will all be fantasy; it is not part of your real world, nor will it ever have to be.

GUIDED IMAGE SCRIPT

Take a moment now to prepare for this visualization . . .
Adjust any clothing that binds you . . .
if you wish, loosen your belt or tie, or remove your shoes . . .
Gently stretch your body and settle into a comfortable position . . .

As you breathe, feel your breath filling your entire body . . .
As you let go of each breath,
feel yourself moving into a relaxed state of consciousness . . .

As you create your relaxed state, close your eyes . . .
and continue your relaxation . . .
feeling yourself becoming quiet and relaxed.

When you are ready . . .
imagine sitting in a comfortable lawn chair in a back yard . . .

⌒ Pause 10 seconds.

Notice the high fence surrounding the yard . . .
no one can see or disturb you . . .
you are peacefully alone with your thoughts . . .

You are enclosed in your imagination . . .
represented by this particular back yard . . .

Just a few feet in front of you is a huge oak tree . . .
focus your attention on the mass of leaves on the tree . . .

⌒ Pause 5 seconds.

As you watch the leaves shimmer in a light breeze,
they seem to blur into a vibrating green mass . . .
and then into a clear empty space . . .
a hole in the fabric of the air . . .

As you watch this gap in space . . .
it becomes a large and perfect circle.

Focus your gaze on this perfect circle
and watch as your fantasy begins to unfold . . .

Just allow your fantasy to come to life
in the frame of this circle
letting the power of your imagination
create whatever fantasy it desires . . .

⌒ Pause 10 seconds.

Observe this creation of your imagination
while allowing all your emotions to emerge freely . . .
and flow into this open space . . .

Trust yourself to view your fantasy fully
with the knowledge that it is safe to do so . . .

Take the time you need to become completely involved . . .

⌒ Pause 90 seconds.

Now it's time for your fantasy to end . . .
Allow the images to play out to their conclusion . . .

⌒ Pause 20 seconds.

And when you are through with your fantasy . . .
continue to gaze into this circle of space . . .
watching it slowly close . . .
and change into a shimmering sea of green leaves . . .

Gradually, the oak tree reappears . . .

Once the tree has become solid . . .
focus your attention on its solid branches and trunk
while you reflect on the fantasy you have just experienced . . .

⤙ Pause 10 seconds.

Consider how the actual fulfillment of your fantasy would affect
your life and the lives of any others this fantasy may include . . .

⤙ Pause 15 seconds.

Ponder over the consequences . . .
all the advantages and disadvantages . . .

⤙ Pause 15 seconds.

When you have reflected upon your fantasy
and its implications . . .
take three long, deep breaths . . .

⤙ Pause 10 seconds.

With the third exhale . . .
open your eyes . . .
and find yourself back where you originally began this exercise.

GROUP PROCESSING OPTION

As a group, discuss how it felt to do the exercise. Was it scary?
Are you comfortable with your decisions about your fantasy?
Do you think the action you lived out in your fantasy is what you
really wanted to do, or symbolic of some other need?

⤙ Explore all safety concerns.

Chapter 8

SCRIPTS *for* CONGRUENCE

The affirming images in this chapter encourage self-awareness,
self-acceptance, and harmony of inner and outer states of being. Participants explore vulnerabilities and strengths as they explore who they
are, how they feel about themselves, how they present themselves to
the world, and the quality of their relationships.

Tree in Winter

Enjoy personal harmony as you visualize
ice melting from tree branches.

GOAL

To promote inner harmony and congruence.

TIME

3 minutes

SPECIAL CONSIDERATIONS

Could be used in almost any group for quick calming.

GUIDED IMAGE SCRIPT

Allow yourself the time now to relax . . . to unwind . . .
to let your mind drift . . . and to let your body float.

Breathe fully and deeply . . . filling your lungs . . .
expanding your belly as you take in air . . . and releasing any
tensions you may have accumulated as you exhale . . .

Gently allow your eyes to close . . .

Pause 10 seconds.

Give yourself permission to have this time . . .
completely without interruptions . . .
without phone calls or distractions . . .
This time is completely yours.

As relaxation naturally takes over your body,
feel the surface upon which your body rests . . .
Settle into this surface . . .
You feel balanced . . .
well-rooted and sturdy in your comfort zone . . .

Pause 5 seconds.

You are deeply relaxed now . . .

Imagine you are the only tree on a small hill . . .
It is just before dawn . . .
and the sun is barely visible over a distant hill . . .

The entire area is covered with a layer of snow . . .
one foot thick . . .
You can feel your branches holding the weight of the snow . . .

    Pause 10 seconds.

It is dawn . . .
and the bright circle of the sun is visible over the distant hill . . .
The sun's rays warm the snow and your branches . . .

    Pause 5 seconds.

Soon, the ice and snow begin to melt and fall off . . .
Your branches are free . . .
Extend them as far as you can . . .

As you stretch your branches . . .
it is time for you to awaken
and stretch your own limbs as well . . .

When you are ready,
you will move from your relaxed position . . .
and stretch your body in any way that feels comfortable . . .
bringing back with you a feeling of freedom and warmth to carry you
through the rest of your day.

    Pause 10 seconds.

Now, open your eyes slowly and let in the sight of the room . . .
You are awake and fully present . . .

GROUP PROCESSING OPTIONS

▓ Repeat the exercise, this time standing up and transforming
yourself into the shape of a tree that moves and stretches in response
to the visualization.

▓ In pairs or small groups brainstorm additional images that would
intesify the impact of this visualization.

Lapping Waves

*Realize self-acceptance and the power of letting go
as you lie in a gently rocking boat.*

GOAL

To relax and experience inner peace.

TIME

2–3 minutes

WARMUP

▨ When we are deeply relaxed, we are generally more open to
ourselves as we really are, without pretenses.

▨ In this state, we increase the potential for self-awareness and
self-understanding.

GUIDED IMAGE SCRIPT

To begin this exercise, gently and slowly tap with your index finger
on any surface around you . . . listen to this sound . . .
and let it rest in your memory for now . . .

↩ *Pause 5 seconds.*

Stop the tapping . . . close your eyes . . .
and make yourself comfortable.

As you close your eyes, let any tension in your body drain out . . .
like water draining out of a basin . . .

Picture your body clear and empty . . .
with great depth and tranquillity . . .

↩ *Pause 5 seconds.*

Similar to the gentle tapping sound your finger made . . .
is the universal sound of water . . .

of waves lapping against a dock . . .
or waves lapping on a sandy beach . . .
or waves lapping against the side of a boat.

Water is an element and sound that soothes, heals and relaxes . . .
Let the sound of lapping waves relax you deeply and completely . . .
Allow your thoughts to drift . . .
until they settle into the slow, gentle sound of waves . . .

You are resting comfortably in the bow of a sturdy boat on a lake . . .
You are becoming more and more relaxed
as you rest your back against the boat's gently curved hull . . .

     Pause 10 seconds.

As the breeze picks up, the rhythm changes . . .
Waves begin to rock the boat gently
and you can hear the water splash against the bow . . .

Your boat is moving steadily forward with the waves . . .
You hear the soft rhythm lapping of the waves . . .
The gentle rolling and lulling sounds bring you into a state of deep,
pleasant relaxation.

     Pause 10 seconds.

As you continue to listen to the sound of the water . . .
allow the motion of the waves to bring you gently back to your
current environment . . .

     Pause 5 seconds.

When you have completely returned from your sailing journey,
you will be awake and refreshed . . .

Return now to the present time . . . awake . . . and refreshed.

GROUP PROCESSING OPTION

    ▨ Reflect on some of the "simple truths" about yourself that you
discover and/or rediscover when you are relaxed. Note two or three of
these personal truths on paper.

    ▨ Share your insights with a partner.

Facial Massage

Dissipate the stress and tension held in your head and face with this simple massage.

GOAL

To experience physical relaxation and mind/body congruence.

TIME

6–8 minutes

SPECIAL CONSIDERATIONS

Appropriate for most groups, although occasionally people who have never learned or used nurturing self-touch may have some anxiety about doing massage.

> ✍ *Even a simple facial massage can to be emotionally painful for abuse victims who have had negative experiences with touch. It also has the potential to be powerful and healing for some individuals. Be ready to offer reassurance and support—and referral when necessary. Processing disturbing memories is best done in therapy groups.*

WARMUP

For many people, the day's stress accumulates in the muscles of the head, face and jaw. A furrowed brow or clenched teeth are sure signs of stress and fatigue.

Massaging your face and head can smooth and relax these tiny muscles, allowing the tension to dissipate.

GUIDED MASSAGE SCRIPT

Place your fingers lightly on your temples . . .
Move your fingers in small, gentle circles for a few minutes . . .

> ✍ *Pause 45 seconds.*

Next . . . move your fingers to your forehead and slowly massage
this area in the same way . . .

⌒ Pause 45 seconds.

Now move to the space right underneath your eyes . . .
Find the two tiny bones jutting out under your eyes . . .
and gently touch them . . . in whatever way feels comfortable.

⌒ Pause 30 seconds.

Next, find one or two *soft spots* located at the base of the rear of the
skull . . . on either side of the upper spinal column . . .
about two inches directly behind the ears . . .
and massage these areas . . .

⌒ Pause 45 seconds.

Now go back and touch each and every part of your face and
head . . . slowly and gently . . .
Remember to do whatever feels good . . .
and pay attention to how you feel . . .

⌒ Pause 60 seconds.

It's time now to finish your last soothing touch . . .
as you finish with your massage, take note of any thoughts, feelings,
or sensations you are experiencing . . .

⌒ Pause 5 seconds.

Now, turn your attention back to the group . . . refreshed and
renewed . . . in touch with yourself.

GROUP PROCESSING OPTION

▧ What particular kinds of touches felt good to you? Describe your
favorites to the group.

*⌒ Encourage group members to give themselves a facial
massage three times in the next week—and to consider
asking a family member for a massage.*

Beach Tides

Affirm your patterns for handling crisis and making decisions in the ebb and flow of your life tides.

GOAL

To increase self-awareness and self-acceptance.

TIME

8–10 minutes

MATERIALS

Recording of ocean waves (optional).

SPECIAL CONSIDERATIONS

A recording of waves crashing on a beach (played at a low yet audible level) will help people visualize this scene.

WARMUP

As a part of the process of living, we experience repetitions, falling into daily routines that make our lives smoother and somewhat predictable.

On a larger scale, we have our own personal style in approaching crises and important decisions.

After undergoing major changes, we fall back into our routine to gather or consolidate our personal resources in a similarly characteristic style.

We even resist major changes in a repetitive way.

This exercise is designed to help us become acutely aware of these repetitions so that we can expand or change the way we experience them or let them go.

Guided Image Script

Sit down comfortably . . .
Close your eyes . . .
Clear your mind . . .
and breathe deeply, slowly and naturally . . .

 Pause 5 seconds.

Gradually relax deeper and deeper . . .
as you tune into the rhythm of your breathing . . .

 Pause 5 seconds.

As you continue to relax into the easy rhythm of your breathing . . .
imagine that you are standing on an ocean beach . . .
listening to the sound of the surf . . .
watching the waves ebb and flow with the rhythm of your breath.

 Pause 10 seconds.

As the scene comes to life in your mind,
pay attention to all the details . . .
Take as much time as you need
to examine every aspect of your beach . . .

Notice everything . . .
Perhaps there are clouds high above . . .
Notice all the details of your beach . . . the sand . . .
rocks . . . dunes . . . beach grass . . . and tidepools . . .

 Pause 10 seconds.

Sniff the salt air . . . and feel the wind as it blows about you . . .
Become comfortable and familiar with the entire setting.

 Pause 15 seconds.

Now allow your gaze
to focus on the movement of the water before you . . .
Watch a wave roll in and fall back . . .
Watch another roll in and fall back . . .
and another . . . and another.

 Pause 15 seconds.

As the waves continue to surge forward and recede . . .
feel the motion lull you with its hypnotic repetition . . .

The motion of the waves
brings to mind the greater motion of the tides . . .
As the waves come in and fall back,
the tide surges in and rolls out . . .

As you continue to focus your attention
on the ebb and flow of the waves . . .
reflect on the much larger *surge* and *retreat* of the great tides . . .
pulled by the moon . . .
and swayed by the motion of the earth . . .
constantly in and out . . . in and out . . .

    Pause 10 seconds.

Now concentrate on the *in* of the wave . . .
Imagine each wave as a tide itself . . .

Focus your attention on what occurs when it comes in . . .
It heaves a little . . . out there in deep water . . .
hardly noticeable except as a moving hump . . .
Then, at a certain point, you notice the wave begin to rise . . .

The wave is gathering up all its hidden power . . .
the force that lay beneath the surface until now . . .
In it comes . . .
growing even bigger . . .

As the wave nears its destination it seems to move faster . . .
Soon you will see it curl over . . .
flash a comb of white . . .
and press in . . . as far onto the sand as it can go . . .

Watch as the wave breaks . . .
and comes rushing in with a final burst of energy . . .
Hear its triumphant sound.

You watch several waves come in this way . . .
Feel each of the stages the wave goes through on its way *in* . . .

    Pause 20 seconds.

As you watch the waves press in . . . allow yourself to remember
a time when you felt like those waves coming *in* . . .
Powerful . . . energetic . . . flowing . . .

    ⟶ *Pause 5 seconds.*

Identify yourself with the waves as you relive this time . . .

Filled with energy . . .
you pull yourself together and rush toward your goal . . .
with high expectations and confidence . . .

You seem to grow physically larger, like the wave . . .

Soon you feel so committed to your goal
that nothing can go wrong . . .
and you cannot consider drawing back . . .

That's when you crest and surge up onto the sand . . .
spending your last ounce of energy and achieving the goal . . .

As you relive this sequence of achievement . . .
identify how the action of the waves coincides with the stages of your
surge toward the goal.

    ⟶ *Pause 10 seconds.*

Now that the wave is high and safe on the beach . . . let your gaze
rest on the highest point the water reaches on the beach . . .

There is a darkened area . . . perhaps even a line . . .
where the water sinks into the thirsty sand . . .

This is where the water stopped and left its mark of
accomplishment . . .
Soon it will have to pull back and regain strength for its next push.

    ⟶ *Pause 5 seconds.*

Now begin to notice the signs that the water is receding . . .
it settles in the tidepools and then drains away . . .
Ridges are etched into the sand
as the water races back out over it . . .

Pebbles clatter back into the surf.

Concentrate on the action of the wave ebbing from the sand . . .

Observe everything that is affected during the going *out* . . .
The sand . . . the rocks . . . the water . . .

⤷ *Pause 20 seconds.*

Other waves are coming in,
but you are focusing on a single wave going *out.*
The water races down the expanse of the beach
out to where it collects itself . . .

As you watch the water go out . . .
allow yourself to remember a time when you did the same . . .

Recall the most recent time when you did this . . .
a time when you were pulling back . . . retreating . . .
because you needed to gather your resources together . . .

Possibly on the defensive . . . a little on edge . . .
you retained some perspective that helped you pull your necessary
resources into yourself . . .

Like the wave, you were going *out* for a time.
Relive this time of gathering energy
as you watch the water recede . . .

⤷ *Pause 20 seconds.*

The water has gone out as far as it must . . .
Focus your attention on the point it has reached . . .

There is a tautness, a coiled energy there . . .
and you feel it inside . . .
a tremendous amount of power is being amassed in one place . . .

Feel that power . . .
Freeze it for a moment . . .
and think about where you would want that energy to go . . .
You are about to let it rush in.

Now imagine all that energy slowly surging in . . .
and then rushing up onto the beach! . . .
You feel it rush in . . . reaching as far as it wants to go . . .
all the way in . . . to its highest point.

⤷ *Pause 10 seconds.*

Now that you have experienced the surge . . .
and the fall-back of your energy with the tides . . .
you are gradually going to return the water to its natural
rhythms . . .

The tides are coming in and going out . . .
and you are watching from your vantage point on the beach . . .

The water is out there, and you are up here . . . safe . . .
breathing easily in your own natural rhythm.

    Pause 10 seconds.

Allow yourself to relax with the entire setting for some time . . .
The beach . . . the soft wind . . . the clouds . . .

    Pause 5 seconds.

When you are ready . . .
open your eyes . . .
relaxed and awake.

GROUP PROCESSING OPTION

Pick a partner and take turns sharing and listening to each other as
you tell about a time when you felt like the wave coming in—
spending your energy with reckless abandon—and a time when you
felt like the wave pulling back—retreating and gathering resources.

Animal Identification

*Explore many dimensions of your personality
as you identify with various animals.*

GOAL

To increase self-awareness and congruence.

TIME

10–12 minutes

SPECIAL CONSIDERATIONS

Useful for work, training, therapy and personal growth groups where self-awareness is a goal. Ideal for groups using theories of Carl Jung, when individuals explore the *shadow side* of their personality (e.g., chaplaincy training groups, spirituality workshops, retreats, dream work).

Since the guided image begins by focusing on a white space, consideration should be given to surroundings, or to having pieces of white paper available for participants. Adjust the first lines of the script as necessary.

WARMUP

This exercise may help you to gain insight into different parts of your personality. You will imagine various animals and you may have different feelings in response to them.

If you do not feel comfortable with any animal, you can send it away and invite a different one to appear. All these animals exist in your imagination, and while they are a part of your subconscious, you are always in control.

GUIDED IMAGE SCRIPT

Begin by focusing your attention on a white spot or surface . . .
(such as a wall, ceiling, or piece of paper . . .)

Stare steadily at the white surface . . .
and as you continue to focus your attention on it . . .
you may find your vision beginning to blur . . .

This blurring phenomenon is quite natural
It is a signal that you are relaxing . . .
and entering a different state of consciousness . . .
one you are creating and controlling . . .

Allow this relaxation to spread throughout your entire body . . .
The more you concentrate, the more relaxed you will feel.

Pause 30 seconds.

Soon your eyes will begin to close . . .
Allow them to close as your body relaxes further . . .
When your eyes are shut . . .
you may see before you the after-image of the white
surface . . . shimmering like a mist . . .

As you focus on the mist, you may notice it expand in all
directions . . . and growing toward you . . .

The mist gradually thickens into a dense fog . . .
The fog provides a sense of concealment and security . . .
and begins to completely envelop you . . .
As this occurs, enjoy this feeling of protection . . .
and relax into the warm embrace of the fog.

Pause 10 seconds.

Soon you will see the fog gradually receding . . . and you will
observe that you are in a forest.
This is your forest . . .
inhabited by a multitude of wildlife . . . all yours . . .

Some trees begin to emerge from the fog . . .
As the fog continues to recede,
it also rises until it stops just above the treetops,
forming a protective bubble that envelops your forest.

Now you survey your domain . . .

Ahead, you see a dark, dense forest of tall trees . . .
When you look behind you,
you see a green, tree-lined mountain rising up into the fog . . .
which hovers over the top half of the mountain . . . cloud-like . . .

When you look to your left,
you see a swamp filled with murky water . . .
and dense, tangled vines . . .

On your right, you see a pleasant, open meadow
of tall, soft, green grass and wildflowers . . .
The meadow is spotted with small pools of clear water . . .

Finally, when you look down a slight distance . . .
you will see a deep hole opening into the earth . . .

Notice your feelings as you survey the different parts of your
domain.

    ↩ *Pause 10 seconds.*

Now it is time to call the animals inhabiting the different parts of
your forest . . .

Direct your gaze upward, toward the sky . . .
Soon, a winged animal flies down out of the sky
and settles on the ground near you . . .
Observe its appearance and behavior as it settles
and notice your response to it . . .

    ↩ *Pause 10 seconds.*

When you have observed the winged animal as much as you wish,
shift your attention to the dark forest in front of you . . .

In this region live the fiercest animals of the forest . . .
As you look toward the forest, remember that you control these
animals . . . You can return any animal to the forest and allow
another to appear.

Now allow a four-legged animal to emerge from the forest . . .
You note its appearance and behavior and your response to it . . .
then you watch as it settles near you . . .

⤿ Pause 10 seconds.

When you feel ready . . .
shift your attention to the sloping mountain behind you . . .
An animal descends from the mountain and settles near you . . .
As it settles nearby, you note its size, shape, and behavior . . .
and your response to it . . .

⤿ Pause 10 seconds.

When you feel that you are finished observing this animal,
you look to your left and view the dark, murky waters
of the swamp . . .
with the gnarled, twisted, densely matted vines . . .

Now an animal emerges from the swampy waters . . .
moving out onto the land and coming to rest nearby . . .
Observe it closely and notice your reactions.

⤿ Pause 10 seconds.

And when you feel ready,
look to your right at the meadow . . .

As you look to your right, you see the peaceful green meadows . . .
with their tall, green grass . . .
and the clear, calm pools.

In these meadows live the tame and friendly animals . . .
Allow one of these animals to emerge from the meadow
and move toward you . . .
until it comes to rest nearby . . .

Note its appearance and behavior . . .
and your response to it . . .

⤿ Pause 10 seconds.

When you are finished observing it,
shift your attention downward . . .
As you look down,
you see the deep, dark hole going far into the earth . . .

Allow an animal to emerge from the hole,
noticing its size, shape, behavior . . . and your response to it.

⤿ Pause 10 seconds.

When you are through observing that animal . . .
survey all the assembled animals . . .
Observe them closely . . . and note your feelings . . .
Do you feel strongly about these animals?

Pause 10 seconds.

Are there any you feel particularly drawn toward?

Pause 10 seconds.

When you have finished observing the animals and your responses to
them . . . focus on the animal from the hole in the earth . . .
and allow it to move back and descend into the dark earth . . .

Pause 5 seconds.

After it has disappeared . . .
focus on the animal from the meadow . . .
Allow it to rise and move toward the meadow . . .
watching until it disappears from sight . . .

Pause 5 seconds.

Now look at the animal from the swamp . . .
Allow it to begin moving back toward the swamp . . .
and follow it with your gaze until it reaches the swamp
and disappears beneath the surface of the water . . .

Pause 5 seconds.

Next, focus your attention on the four-legged animal from the
forest . . .
Watch it rise and move into the dark forest,
until it disappears . . .

Pause 5 seconds.

Then shift your gaze to the winged animal . . .
Allow it to rise and fly upward . . .
watching it until it disappears behind the thick white fog above . . .

Pause 5 seconds.

As you look upward at the sky . . .
you will see the protective bubble of fog
gradually begin to lower . . .

expanding and growing denser and denser . . .
enveloping the treetops once again.

Soon, you can see only the dim outline of your forest through the thickening fog . . .

Now you see the fog thicken around you
until it completely envelops you . . .

You feel protected by the fog . . .
Safe and secure . . .

When you feel ready to leave the forest,
the fog will begin to lift, replaced by a refreshing, hazy mist.

Take a moment to relax in the forest . . .
reflecting on your experience . . .

　　Pause 15 seconds.

Now it is time to leave the forest . . .
Imagine yourself fading with the dissipating fog . . .
and coming back to the here and now . . .

　　Pause 5 seconds.

Ready to make this transition back to the present,
you may awaken and open your eyes.

GROUP PROCESSING OPTION

▧ Jot down your responses to the imagery.

Which animal was most like you and why? Which animal was the least like you and why? Which animal could teach you the most and why?

Did any of the animals or any of your responses to them surprise you? Did you feel any particular animal react strongly toward you, positively or negatively?

▧ Share your discoveries with your small group.

Gifts

*Envision perfect gifts to give and receive
in this celebration of intimacy.*

GOAL

To heighten self-awareness and self-acceptance.

TIME

12–15 minutes

SPECIAL CONSIDERATIONS

Ideal for more intimate groups such as couples or communication
workshops. Also appropriate for assertiveness training classes during a
discussion of giving and receiving as an assertive skill.

WARMUP

▨ Giving and receiving gifts can be gestures loaded with significance.
A thoughtfully-chosen gift reflects our feelings for the other person,
our judgment of his or her desires, and perhaps our hopes for the
future of the relationship.

▨ Ideally, when choosing a meaningful gift, we use a sensitive
combination of memory and intuition.

▨ The same holds true in reverse. When someone gives us a gift, we
may learn new things about the giver's perception of us and their
expectations for the subsequent course of the relationship.

▨ In this exercise, through the imagery of gift giving, we are going to
concentrate on our feelings and concerns for those to whom we feel
closest.

*⤳ Before starting the visualization allow preparation time
for group participants to recall past gifts they have given to
and received from special people in their lives. It might be
helpful for people to jot down a few notes on paper.*

GUIDED IMAGE SCRIPT

Start by breathing deeply and completely . . .
feeling the air fill your lungs and release through your nose . . .

↩ Pause 10 seconds.

Begin this visualization by thinking about a beautiful bow topping
off the perfect gift wrapping . . .
Notice the color of the bow . . .
and the texture of the ribbon . . .

↩ Pause 5 seconds.

In your mind's eye,
slowly follow the bow around all of its edges . . .
Like the figure eight, trace it around and around . . .
several times . . .

As you visually trace this shape . . .
feel yourself relax . . .
And when you have finished following the edge of the bow
around . . . in your mind's eye . . . eight times . . .
close your eyes.

↩ Pause 10 seconds.

Take a few moments to remember gifts you have presented to people
in the past . . .

Some of these gifts may have been given on formal or specific
occasions . . .
perhaps others you presented just because it felt right . . .

Recall the process of choosing the most appropriate gift . . .
how you chose it, and how the recipient felt.

↩ Pause 10 seconds.

Now you are going to choose the ideal gifts for two people to whom
you feel close . . .
Geographical distance from them is irrelevant . . .
but it would be preferable to choose people whose relationship to you
is different . . .
such as mother and friend . . . or co-worker and uncle . . .
rather than two siblings.

You are going to choose the perfect gift for each of these people . . .

It does not have to be a tangible item . . .
You may choose to give a character trait that each one has always lacked or desired . . .
Perhaps the gift of time for a crucial period in the person's life would be most appropriate . . .

Be as creative as possible in choosing an appropriate gift for these individuals to express your feelings for them . . .

You cannot give the same gift to both people.

Let's begin with the first person you have chosen . . .
Person A . . .

Allow yourself to meditate for a moment on your knowledge of and experiences with Person A . . .
Think about your first meeting . . .
your shared experiences . . .
his or her greatest frustrations and sources of happiness.

    Pause 15 seconds.

You are actually going to give Person A two different gifts . . .
the first gift will represent your best choice of what you think Person A *wants* most . . .

Consider who and where this person is . . .
compared to where he or she wants to be in life . . .

Take all the time you need to make your choice . . .
remember, what the person *wants* may or may not be in his or her best interest.

    Pause 15 seconds.

The second part of your gift represents what you feel Person A *needs* . . .

You have already given the person what you think he or she wants . . .
what you think the person *needs* may be quite different . . .

Consider emotional . . . physical . . . social . . . and professional concerns . . .

Perhaps your gift will take the form of a small resource that will enable Person A to get what he or she needs.

Once again, take all the time that is necessary for you to choose a gift that will best suit this person's needs.

✍ *Pause 15 seconds.*

Now that you have chosen gifts for Person A,
you will switch roles . . .
Person A is going to choose gifts for *you* . . .

First, imagine that person choosing what he or she thinks you might *want* . . .

You will have to imagine how Person A sees you and how much you have talked to this person about your desires . . .

Think about what Person A would give you if that friend really wanted to please you.

✍ *Pause 15 seconds.*

The second part of the gift will probably be more challenging . . .
It is always harder to know what *we* need
than to know what our friends need.

Now we are going to go a step further . . .
choose the gift that Person A would pick for you if Person A were going to give you what he or she thought you *needed* . . .

Again, this means assessing your relationship from the other person's point of view . . .
and attempting to identify what your friend might recommend for you that would make your life more complete.

✍ *Pause 15 seconds.*

You have now chosen a two-fold gift for Person A . . .
The first part supplies your friend's desire . . .
and a second part answers your friend's needs . . .
Then you have imagined that person doing the same for you.

Now we will go through the same process with the second person you chose at the beginning of this exercise . . .

Allow yourself to meditate on your knowledge and experience
of Person B for a moment . . .

Think about how you met this person . . .
what you know of his or her past . . .
the experiences you shared . . .
and Person B's greatest frustrations . . .
as well as sources of happiness.

Now consider the first part of your gift . . .
your choice for what your friend *wants* . . .

Take all the time you need to make your choice.

    ↜ *Pause 15 seconds.*

The second part of your gift represents what you believe
Person B *needs* . . .
Again, keep in mind that you might better serve his or her best
interests by bestowing some quality or resource that would enable
your friend to move forward . . .
rather than giving an object or static situation intended to create
instant happiness . . .

Once again, take as much time as you need to choose a gift that will
best suit your friend's needs.

    ↜ *Pause 15 seconds.*

Now that you have chosen gifts for Person B,
it is time for Person B to return the favor . . .

First, imagine that person choosing something to please *you* . . .

    ↜ *Pause 15 seconds.*

Person B's second gift represents what he or she thinks you *need* . . .
Again, this means assessing your relationship from the other person's
point of view.

    ↜ *Pause 15 seconds.*

You have completed a wonderful ritual . . .

As you complete this experience,
take your time contemplating what has transpired . . .

holding on to the memories and feelings of this experience . . .
as you return your awareness to the group and your surroundings.

↪ *Pause 5 seconds.*

Focus now on your breathing . . .
and on the count of three, it is time to return . . .

One . . . two . . . three.

Awaken and open your eyes.

GROUP PROCESSING OPTION

▨ Which gift that you presented gave you the most pleasure? Which gift that you received gave you the most pleasure? Describe them both to your small group.

HOMEWORK

▨ Find a time in the next week to discuss with a partner, family member, or close friend what your ideas for two perfect gifts for them would be, and then ask them to tell you what their ideas for two perfect gifts for you would be. Take advantage this opportunity to expand your understanding of your wants and needs as well as your awareness of how others see you.

Corridor of Time

Rediscover life meaning as you explore connections to ancestors, your cultural heritage, and the future world.

GOAL

To enhance self-esteem.

TIME

10–12 minutes

SPECIAL CONSIDERATIONS

Ideal for groups celebrating and affirming cultural diversity, or for classes studying these issues.

Not very well-suited for people in later years (85 years and older) because of the twenty-year projection into the future. Shorten this timespan as appropriate to the age of your group.

WARMUP

▨ With this visualization you will experience the past and future, and explore the impact of your life on those around you.

▨ As you imagine traveling back through time, you may find yourself playing a part in your ancestral past. Then, by coming forward in time at an accelerated speed, you will travel twenty years into your future and discover the impact your life has made.

GUIDED IMAGE SCRIPT

Stretch a bit and get comfortable as you begin to relax . . .

Close your eyes . . . and take three deep breaths . . .
allowing your body to become more and more relaxed . . .
as you breathe in slowly . . . and exhale completely.

⤿ *Pause 10 seconds.*

As you continue to relax, allow your mind to empty . . .
letting go of worries or concerns . . . thoughts . . . and images . . .
until your mind is clear.

    Pause 10 seconds.

Slowly allow a large mirror to take form in your mind's eye.
Look into the mirror . . . and study yourself intently . . .

And, after getting a clear image . . .
consider how you feel about what you see . . .

    Pause 10 seconds.

Keeping this image in mind,
visualize yourself standing between two mirrors . . .
one in front of you and one behind . . .
to create a feeling of three-dimensional depth . . .

You can see your face duplicated many times . . .
getting smaller and smaller in the distance . . .

You also see multiple images of the back of your head receding into
the depths of a tunnel of mirrors . . .

    Pause 5 seconds.

Slowly take a deep breath
while studying your features up close again . . .
As you scan your face, look for signs of your heritage . . .
any distinct features that might link you to distant ancestors . . .

Perhaps you may detect hints of Native American, African, Asian,
Slavic, Latin, or Irish features . . .
or other possible connections to the past . . .

As you note these aspects of your heritage,
allow yourself to drift slowly backward . . .
using the corridor of mirrors to take you to a time and place from
which your ancestors came . . .

Drifting back in time . . .
feel yourself become a part of this past . . .
Those features of your face that were just hints of an older culture
stand out prominently now.

You may begin to feel the clothing and jewelry of that period adorn your body . . .

Inside, feel the sense of community and the spiritual force that your ancestors shared among one another . . .

    Pause 5 seconds.

As you approach the end of the corridor,
glance at your surroundings . . .

What sort of land is this? . . .
What light and weather patterns grace this older part of the world? . . .
Do you know where you are? . . .
Do you live in a society of some kind? . . .
What kind of people do you see around you?

Take an inventory of this culture and its people . . .
merely observing . . . without judging anything or anyone . . .

    Pause 15 seconds.

Once you have understood where you are in space and time,
allow yourself to examine the role you have in this society . . .

Are you the same sex? . . . Are you alone? . . .
What responsibilities do you have? . . .
Do you recognize the clothing you wear or does it surprise you?

Take time to explore the past and feel comfortable being a part of it.

    Pause 20–30 seconds.

Now it is approaching the time to leave . . .
Knowing this, take a last look around . . . remembering everything you witnessed and participated in . . . knowing that you can come back through the corridor to this older place at another time . . .

Stretch a bit and take a deep breath as you look again into the mirrors and journey forward in time to the present . . .

As you travel through the corridor, imagine that your ancestral garb is falling away to reveal your everyday clothing . . .
and you regain your familiar physical identity . . .

    Pause 5 seconds.

When you have returned to the here and now . . .
you have become the same person you were prior to the beginning of
this exercise.

Take a deep breath, and while exhaling, open your eyes . . .

Become familiar with yourself and your present surroundings . . .
Reassure your conscious and subconscious mind that you are in fact
back in the present . . .

Reflect on your unique experience in the past . . .
Try not to hold onto anything for too long or to intellectualize . . .
for in a few moments, you will go on . . .

    Pause 20 seconds.

As soon as you are convinced that you are once again yourself . . .
take a deep breath . . . close your eyes . . .
and allow yourself to drift into a still deeper state of relaxation . . .
preparing to continue your journey . . .

This time, you will be exploring your future . . .
twenty years from now.
As with the journey into the past, don't judge what you may live
through, so that you can experience it more fully.
Once again visualize yourself standing between two mirrors . . .
gazing at your reflections stretching into infinity . . .

    Pause 5 seconds.

Now, take a deep breath, relax . . .
and as you exhale, feel yourself pulled forward into the future . . .
beckoned through the corridor of time . . .

You may recognize this pull as currents of air pressing against you
and then passing you by . . .
Shadows flit over your face, and you feel your body settle more
comfortably into itself as the years pass . . .
Gradually the process slows and you come to a halt . . .

You have now traveled twenty years ahead . . .
You are located somewhere in the future.

As you traveled through these twenty years at high speed,
your life was affected by everyone and everything around you . . .

causing and responding to thousands of events . . .
Some were minor changes . . .
Some significantly altered the lives of others . . .
One or two may have involved earthshaking events . . .

Before you actually survey this future,
reflect on all the people whose lives touched yours in the past . . .
and all the doors that could have opened now in the years ahead.

Which people will have remained in your life? . . .
Who will have played an even bigger role than in the past? . . .
What do you think you will be doing?

    Pause 20 seconds.

Once you have considered the possibilities, take a look at your
surroundings . . .
What sort of light and weather do you find yourself in? . . .
Is this a rural or urban setting? . . .
Do you feel entirely comfortable here in the future?

    Pause 10 seconds.

Now consider yourself in this time and place . . .
What clothing are you wearing? . . .
Are you alone? . . . What do you do in this world? . . .
When you think back, over your life, what changes are appar-
ent? . . .
Which goals have you achieved?
Most important, think about how your actions and accomplishments
may have changed the lives of others and the world around you . . .

    Pause 20 seconds.

Now, try to imagine this future without your presence . . .
as if you were not a part of it all . . .
How does that change this future setting? . . .
Who will have missed you? . . .
Will your absence have made a difference in the lives of people who
knew you? . . .

Is there someone special in your current life . . . or someone you
may want in your life? . . . Think of that someone . . .
If you disappeared from the present, how would that person prosper

in this world? . . .
Where would that person be twenty years in the future?

⤙ Pause 10 seconds.

Reflect a moment longer before beginning the journey back to the present . . .

⤙ Pause 5 seconds.

Take a deep breath and allow yourself to ease back into the corridor. You are leaving the future . . . but taking your observations and making them a part of you . . .

Once again, you feel the breeze of time passing swiftly . . . Notice the flitting shadows . . . and feel your body readjust . . .

As you near the here and now . . . you feel more in contact with your body . . . and become your present self once again . . . feeling relaxed . . .

You arrive at the present with a newly-gained recognition of your importance and role in life . . .

Take another moment to reflect on your experiences in the future . . .

⤙ Pause 5 seconds.

Exhale . . . and now open your eyes.

GROUP PROCESSING OPTION

▨ Share with the group some part of your experience with the past in this visualization. What time period did you visit? What geographical location? Whom did you meet?

⤙ Record these answers on newsprint as people describe their journeys. Draw out and affirm diversity in the group.

▨ As you traveled to the future, what did you notice as your unique contributions to the world? Share with the large group.

Chapter 9

SCRIPTS *for* CLARITY

The challenging images in this chapter generate mental and spiritual clarity—a heightened awareness of what is important and meaningful. Participants sift and sort, embracing and discarding, exploring options for creating an environment that reflects their identity and values.

Awakening Lawn

Rake away the debris from your mental lawn,
leaving the landscape ready for growth and new life.

GOAL

To foster increased mental and spiritual clarity.

TIME

3–4 minutes

SPECIAL CONSIDERATIONS

Ideal for workshops focused on change, values clarification, or
personal/organizational renewal.

GUIDED IMAGE SCRIPT

The cycle of nature always allows for new growth . . .

Settle back and relax now
as you prepare for a new phase in your own growth cycle . . .
beginning with the natural, relaxing cycle of breathing . . .

Inhale and exhale completely . . .

    ↩ *Pause 5 seconds.*

On the next breath, mentally count to *four* as you inhale slowly
and as you slowly exhale, mentally count to *six* . . .
releasing all the toxins with your breath.
Inhale to four counts . . . Exhale to six . . .

Continue this relaxing breathing cycle for three more breaths . . .
and with the third exhale, allow your eyes to close . . .

    ↩ *Watch and listen to participants breathe. Pause until*
    most have finished three breaths and closed their eyes.

Continue to focus on your breathing . . .
with your eyes closed now, deepening your relaxation . . .

Inhale and exhale completely . . .

⌇ Pause 5 seconds.

On the next relaxing breath,
mentally count to *six* as you inhale slowly . . .
and as you slowly exhale, mentally count to *eight* . . .
releasing any remaining tension with your breath . . .

Continue this relaxing breathing cycle for three more breaths . . .

⌇ Pause 15 seconds.

As your relaxation continues,
think about winter . . .
Most everything alive slows down . . .
hibernates . . .
and sleeps . . .

⌇ Pause 5 seconds.

As with all seasons, change is imminent . . .
and winter will soon be over . . .

The new season is here . . .

It is a warm spring day . . .
and you are about to rake your lawn in order to awaken it . . .
It has been matted and frozen all winter.

In slow, steady strokes you rake through the lawn . . .
removing all the dry yellow strands of grass . . .
and cleaning any litter and leaves that have accumulated . . .

The grass begins to breathe as your raking opens, clears,
and refreshes . . .
making way for new life to grow.

You have begun to accomplish a dramatic cleaning
and achieve a significant change . . .

⌇ Pause 5 seconds.

As this transformation continues . . .
it is time for you to return to the present . . .
time to bring your anticipation for renewal and growth . . .
into your current life . . .

AWAKENING LAWN

Focus on your breathing . . .
just as you did to begin this exercise . . .

Inhale slowly as you mentally count to *four* . . .
And as you exhale,
let your breath out slowly as you mentally count to *six* . . .

> ✍ *Pause 5 seconds.*

Continue breathing in this way . . .
slowly and deeply . . .
and after three complete inhalations and exhalations . . .
you are ready to open your eyes and awaken.

> ✍ *Allow enough time to complete this breathing
> sequence before intruding.*

GROUP PROCESSING OPTION

▓ Write about some of the "dead matter" that you would like to rake
out of your life. This could be physical, mental, spiritual, social, or
emotional matter.

> ✍ *Encourage people to write quickly without censoring
> their thoughts. Caution people not to judge themselves or
> others.*

▓ Look over your list and choose one "dead matter" item you
definitely want to change. Find a partner and compare notes.

Neck Stretch

*Refresh your mind and body with this
stretch for the deskbound.*

GOAL

To relax tense muscles in the neck area.

TIME

3 minutes

SPECIAL CONSIDERATIONS

A good warmup or quick energizer for most groups.

> ✍ *Demonstrate the stretches as you give verbal instructions. Remind participants this is not a competition. They should stretch gently, and never push to the point of pain.*

GUIDED STRETCH SCRIPT

Begin by sitting in a comfortable upright chair.

Look straight ahead, with your knees together . . .

Grasp the underside of the chair seat . . .
and pull upwards on the seat,
at the same time you lower both shoulders a few inches . . .

Your elbows, by this time, should be slightly bent.

As you pull up on the chair . . . you should feel the muscles
between your neck and shoulders stretch . . .

These are the long muscles running from the top of your shoulders
to the back of your neck, called the *trapezius* muscles . . .

Next, simply rotate your head from left to right . . .
and to the left again . . .
as if you were shaking your head *no* . . .

Do *not* "help" your stretch by pushing your head with your hands. This may result in an injury.

Instead, place your hands on the sides of your neck . . . so you can gently massage the two areas being stretched . . .

Keep breathing throughout your stretch . . .

When you are done with your stretch, take note of any thoughts . . . feelings . . . and sensations you are experiencing . . .

    ↬ *Pause 5 seconds.*

When you have noted these, you have completed this exercise for now.

GROUP PROCESSING OPTION

▨ Stand up and stretch any other part of your body that feels tense. Move around the room as you do these extra stretches.

▨ After a minute or two, find a partner and compare notes about where you typically hold tension in your body and what you do to relieve it.

Vacation Spot

*Relax completely on a mental holiday to a place
free from distractions and responsibilities.*

GOAL
To foster relaxation and mental clarity.

TIME
4–6 minutes

SPECIAL CONSIDERATIONS
Appropriate for almost any group, including worksite groups and
wellness programs, teaching the importance of a mental get-away for
relaxation, refocusing, and renewal.

GUIDED IMAGE SCRIPT
Allow yourself to get comfortable . . .
loosen any constricting clothing or shoes . . .

Remember a time when you felt truly relaxed and content . . .
peaceful and calm . . .

Breathe deeply as you reflect upon these special moments.

    ↩ *Pause 15 seconds.*

Breathe deeply and allow yourself to drift mentally to your favorite
vacation spot . . .
one you've been to before,
or a new one . . .
or even an imaginary vacation spot . . .

Allow your breath and relaxation to carry you to this special
place . . .

Your favorite vacation spot could be a secluded forest cabin . . .
or a geodesic dome containing a miniature world floating in space.

It could be a vacant island beach . . . or a local park bench.

You need not be in an exotic place to relax . . .

Let your eyes close and in your mind's eye,
picture this special spot . . .

Notice everything about it,
bringing to your mind everything associated with it . . .

↪ *Pause 20–30 seconds.*

Now, step into the picture.

Relax . . . as you settle comfortably into this place.

↪ *Pause 10 seconds.*

Imagine the view from this place . . .
the smells . . .
the people around you . . .
the temperature . . .
what you are wearing . . .
and especially how clear and lucid you feel while here . . .

↪ *Pause 20–30 seconds.*

There are no deadlines here . . .
no responsibilities . . .
or unwelcome intrusions.

Perhaps your most pressing worry is whether or not you have the
right sunscreen on . . .
or perhaps you're wondering why you don't come here more
often . . .

↪ *Pause 10 seconds.*

Harness this relaxed feeling . . .
You have the innate ability to carry it with you
on your journey back home . . .

Keep this relaxed feeling as you awaken . . .
and hold onto your vacation
as a permanent attitude which you carry around . . .

↪ *Pause 10 seconds.*

Now it is time to re-emerge and awaken . . .
bringing the peace and refreshment of your vacation
back within you.

GROUP PROCESSING OPTION

Pick a partner and describe your vacation spot in detail to the other person. Describe what values are clearest to you when you're in this spot.

Reverse roles, and have your partner describe his or her vacation spot and values connected to this space.

Money

Spend ten billion dollars to discover your priorities.

GOAL

To clarify goals and values.

TIME

8–10 minutes

MATERIALS

Paper and pencils; jewels such as gems, cut crystal, or rhinestones (optional).

SPECIAL CONSIDERATIONS

People may find it helpful to have a pad of paper and pencil to jot down ideas as they go through the visualization.

Some people may find it easier to get involved in this visualization if they have actual jewels (gems, crystals, rhinestones) to use as a focal point.

WARMUP

Some people say the world revolves around relationships, others say around money. Is money the "root of all evil?"

Whether you are inclined to think so or not, money is an important reality for all of us. Finances affect the decisions we make, the course of our human relationships, and the quality of our lives.

It's hard for most people to say what they would do with great wealth when they've never had it.

In this visualization you are going to control a tremendous amount of money to see how you would handle it. The decisions you make about its use should suggest something about your goals and values.

GUIDED IMAGE SCRIPT

To begin, simply place your palms face up in your lap . . .
open your hands fully . . . and feel their weight and warmth . . .
Gently wiggle your fingers . . . then let them relax and curl to a
more naturally comfortable position . . .

Close your eyes . . .
You find yourself relaxing more and more . . .
deeper and deeper with each passing moment . . .

   Pause 10 seconds.

Imagine that you are holding a fantastic precious jewel . . .
a ruby or a diamond or a rare crystal . . .
Stare deeply at the gem in your mind's eye . . . paying attention to
the way it glitters . . . and the number and angles of its facets . . .

Think carefully about the gem's value to society . . .
While you continue to take deep, relaxing breaths . . .

   Pause 10 seconds.

As you allow your surroundings to come into focus . . .
you find yourself gazing upon the jewel in your hand
while sitting behind a massive desk . . .
You are on the sixty-second floor of a modern skyscraper . . .
To your right is a large picture window through which you can see
the city far below.

As you turn over the precious stone in your hand, contemplate your
position as president and sole proprietor of a massive fund worth ten
billion dollars . . .

Ask yourself: "What is ten billion dollars?"
It's a thousand dollars times a thousand times a thousand again . . .
and that amount ten more times . . . It represents more than twice
as many dollars as there are human beings on the planet . . .
If you laid ten billion dollar bills end to end, they would stretch to
the moon, back to earth, to the moon a second time, and halfway
home again.

The money is safely deposited in the bank many floors below your
office . . . A treasurer, an accountant, and numerous other people
work for you and will make investments, purchases, gifts, or

donations with this money any time you wish . . .

You could invest in a number of things . . . You could buy anything you desire . . . You could attempt to gain leverage over other people, organizations, or countries . . . You could even give it all away.

Pause 10 seconds.

As you sit there musing on the possibilities, the intercom on your desk buzzes softly . . . Your administrative assistant's voice enters the room . . . "What do you want me and your other employees to do today?" he asks.

It is time to go to work . . . You have to organize your daydreams and decide what you wish to accomplish today . . . Through your choices . . . with this wealth at your disposal . . . you are going to facilitate a number of actions.

Carefully consider your first instruction to your administrative assistant, and then tell him your decision . . .

Pause 15 seconds.

As he notifies the other employees who will disburse the funds and make sure the money is properly distributed, contemplate what you have done . . .
Allow yourself to think about how you feel about this decision . . .
Consider how it might affect the other people's lives . . .
Consider how it will affect you, and the course of your own life.

Pause 20 seconds.

Your assistant comes back on the intercom,
asking for your next instruction . . .
You pick up a pen and write down three to five other things you wish to do with your money today . . .

Pause 15 seconds.

After you've chosen a number of significant projects,
you put them in order of importance . . .

Pause 10 seconds.

Next you take the first project on your list and give your assistant his next instruction . . . He takes several moments to contact the appropriate people who will get the job done . . .

Again you muse upon the ramifications of your decision . . .
How does it make you feel to have done this? . . . How will it affect
your life, the lives of other people, the course of events in general?

 ⌒ *Pause 15 seconds.*

Perhaps you think of another task you would like to accomplish . . .
one that is more meaningful
than some or all of the others on your list . . .
You jot it down on the note pad and await the voice of your assistant.

 ⌒ *Pause 15 seconds.*

Your assistant comes on again and you give him your next
instruction . . . He makes the necessary arrangements as you
imagine what effects your decision will have upon the people you
know, yourself, and the world at large . . .

Pay particular attention to the way you feel about the fact that you
are exerting power to effect changes in accord with your desires . . .
How does it feel to have such power, and to know your decisions will
be carried out?

 ⌒ *Pause 10 seconds.*

While you are concentrating on this, you will slowly become aware
of the gem in your hand . . . You turn it around three times . . .
On the third rotation, you will awaken . . . and return to the
present.

 ⌒ *Allow plenty of time for people to end their own
visualization (20–60 seconds).*

GROUP PROCESSING OPTION

▓ Reflect on your spending decisions in the guided imagery. Are you
satisfied with them? Surprised by them? Regretful about them? Were
there any decisions you would prefer to take back now? Are there any
others you wish you would have made instead?

▓ Share with a partner how you spent the money, and how you felt
about your decisions.

Dream House

*Create an expansive imaginary home that is a
true reflection of your identity and lifestyle.*

GOAL

To identify and clarify values.

TIME

12–14 minutes

MATERIALS

Large sheets of large newsprint and colored markers (if Group
Processing Option is used).

SPECIAL CONSIDERATIONS

This exercise is highly open-ended and adaptable for different
audiences. The text includes questions that provide springboards for
your creativity. Once you've read through the exercise you may
change its order, reject any suggestions, or break it up, taking several
sessions to complete it.

WARMUP

One of the inescapable facts of creativity, whether you make a
sculpture or a mental image, is that whatever you create expresses
some mixture of your background, perceptions, and desires.

In this exercise, you will design a house that meets all your ideal
specifications. In the course of laying out a floor plan and furnishing
each room, you may see a reflection of yourself as you would like to
be.

Before you begin to construct your perfect house, bear in mind
that you will probably move very slowly through this image, as you
will have to create each and every item along the way.

Guided Image Script

↝ *Move slowly through the script, making sure people have enough time to create each item as they go.*

Begin by thinking about your present home . . .
Decide which aspects are positive and which are inadequate . . .
As you look around, slowly take three deep breaths . . .

↝ *Pause 10 seconds.*

On your third exhalation, finish your survey . . .
Allow your eyes to close . . . and let your breath carry you to the site of your dream house . . . a perfect home of your own design . . .
a home you are going to build in your imagination . . .

Your dream house can be as large or as small . . .
cluttered or bleak . . . conservative or bizarre as you like . . .

You will be able to create the structure and its components instantly from your own mental storehouse . . .
You can can include whatever features you can imagine . . .
whether they are "typical" or unconventional . . .

First, you must decide upon a shape . . .
Perhaps you stroll around the outside of the house to establish its basic outline and size . . .
You consider the size . . . type of frame . . . building materials . . . and color.

↝ *Pause 10 seconds.*

Before stepping inside, mentally catalog all the rooms you want to have in your house . . .
You may choose to include a porch . . . foyer . . . living room . . .
dining room . . . kitchen . . . pantry . . . study . . .
bathrooms . . . bedrooms . . . recreation rooms . . . hobby rooms . . . greenhouse . . . indoor or outdoor balconies . . .
attic . . . basement . . . garage . . . music room . . . whatever you choose . . .

If you wish, you could combine the functions of two or more rooms into a single space . . .
or create your own room designed for specific activities such as sewing or lifting weights.

↜ *Pause 10 seconds.*

As you choose and design your rooms, picture their position in relationship to each other . . . their size in relationship to the others . . . the number of floors they will occupy . . . and the rooms that are on each floor . . .

↜ *Pause 10 seconds.*

Don't overexert yourself with this initial planning, since you are about to step into your house and create each feature in detail as you walk through it . . .

Now, find yourself standing before the entrance to your dream house . . .

Decide on the size and design of your entry
and whether you want to have a door . . .
If there is a door, what does it look like? . . .
You may install a knocker, handle, or bell . . .
There may be a way for people to look in or out through it . . .
Consider what else you might like to add to this entrance that would suggest something about the person who lives inside.

↜ *Pause 20 seconds.*

Once you have designed an entrance, you are ready to step inside.

Step inside . . . look around . . .
and decide whether you want to create a foyer . . . a hallway . . .
or a full-fledged room of the house . . .

↜ *Pause 20 seconds.*

Notice the type of lighting that illuminates this area . . .
Is it artificial or natural? . . . Adjust it to suit you . . .
Are there any knickknacks in this area?
Are there any closets or places to hang coats?

↜ *Pause 20 seconds.*

What lies beyond the entry way? . . .

Slowly scan this room and take in its size and shape . . .
Look at the floor . . . Is it covered or bare? . . .
Notice the height of the ceiling . . .

and the type of lighting, if any, in this room . . .
Choose the furnishings that please you . . . furniture . . .
plants . . . glassware . . . devices or equipment . . .
and decorations . . .

If you choose a design you later find you dislike,
you can reshape the room at any time.

Pause 30 seconds.

Once you feel that you have spent sufficient time in the first room . . . move on to another.

Where will you eat? . . . Do you have a dining room? . . .
If so, conduct an inventory . . .

Choose a floor and furnishings . . .
Settle on the lighting you want to accompany meals . . .
Perhaps you will want to include artwork in the room.

Pause 30 seconds.

As soon as you are satisfied with the dining area,
consider where your food will be prepared.

Choose the major and minor appliances you want and decide where they are going to be kept . . . Does this space have any other special items to make food preparation easier? . . .

What do the floors, walls, and ceiling look like? . . .

Pause 30 seconds.

When you have designed this area, think about where you will sleep.
What does it look like? . . .

Are there provisions for keeping warm, or do you even need any?
Are there windows or an access to the outside?
Are there other sleeping areas in the house?

Pause 20 seconds.

Another possible convenience would be the bathroom . . .
Choose a location. Or more than one.

What colors predominate? . . .
What do the bathing facilities include? . . .

Observe the type and placement of toilets . . .
sinks . . . mirrors . . . tubs or showers . . .
cupboards . . . shelves . . .
and whatever else appears in your bathrooms.

↬ *Pause 20 seconds.*

So far you have constructed only the basic rooms of your house . . .
You may even have decided not to include some of them within your
space.

Remember, you are in control here,
and you are free to choose exactly what you want.

If some of the suggestions don't fit your mental picture,
throw them out.
If you want anything that isn't mentioned,
simply wish it into your dream house.

Now it's time to let your imagination run wild and finish building.

Perhaps your house has a study . . .
consider its uses and furnish it accordingly.

↬ *Pause 20 seconds.*

Maybe you desire a recreation room . . . a greenhouse . . .
a back porch . . . an attic . . . a basement . . . a workshop . . . a
library . . . or an indoor tennis court.

↬ *Pause 10 seconds.*

Take the time you need to identify the rooms you want . . .
Place each one in your dream house . . .
and then furnish it however you want.

↬ *Pause 60 seconds.*

Do you have any other rooms?

Where are they located and what do they look like?

↬ *Pause 20 seconds.*

Now that you have established each room in your house,
take some time to wander back through them . . .

and see that all is as you would have it . . .

You may improve upon anything or eliminate it . . .
but make sure you feel completely satisfied with your house and
have not forgotten anything.

    ✍ *Pause 60 seconds.*

Take a few more moments to explore your house . . .
you may wish to revisit your favorite room for a few more moments.

    ✍ *Pause 30 seconds.*

Now, on the count of three . . .
you will awaken . . .
and find yourself back in your own surroundings . . .

Ready?

One . . . two . . . three.

Once you are awake . . .
take a few moments to mentally review your imaginary house
and its various rooms . . .
knowing you may revisit your house often to take inventory
and to redesign or refurbish it according to your desires.

GROUP PROCESSING OPTION

▨ Use newsprint and markers to draw a floor plan of your ideal
home, including all the rooms you created.

    ✍ *Allow time for people to add important details, colors
or decorations. Some people may want to sketch the view
of the outside of the house as well.*

▨ Describe your favorite room to your partner or small group.

    ✍ *Participants could lay out (or hang on the wall) all
the floor plans and let group members walk on a "tour of
homes" to see each other's dream house.*

Tornado

*Sweep up the baggage of your life in a
whirlwind of spiritual housecleaning.*

GOAL

To clarify priorities and values.

TIME

8–10 minutes

SPECIAL CONSIDERATIONS

Especially relevant for groups where people are dealing with life
transitions and/or crises, or for workplaces undergoing major
changes.

May be done outdoors if the group is small.

WARMUP

▓ A tornado is one of nature's most powerful forces. We tend to
think of it as destructive because it tears down large objects in its path
and sweeps away smaller ones. Yet, in another sense, a tornado may
be looked at as a force that reveals the temporary nature of human
structures. Nothing, no matter how immovable and permanent it
may seem, can stand unchanged in its path.

▓ At times we all feel the need for a "spiritual house cleaning." In this
exercise you will imagine gathering all your energy into a huge
tornado that will rearrange your affairs and put you more in touch
with your higher self. Some of the objects and activities may not
necessarily apply to you, depending upon your age and lifestyle.
Concentrate on the references that apply directly to you.

GUIDED IMAGE SCRIPT

*⌒ Be sure to read this script slowly enough to allow
participants to identify specifics about their lives.*

As you prepare for this inner journey . . .
relax into your surroundings . . .
Tune into the rhythm of your body . . . the gentle flow of your
breath . . . the steady beat of your heart . . . and the natural stretch
and relaxation of your muscles . . .

    Pause 10 seconds.

As you relax more and more deeply into the quiet space around you
and within you . . .
close your eyes and allow your mind's eye to open . . .
Picture yourself walking into an open field on a sunny day . . .
with a few billowing clouds overhead . . .
and a light breeze blowing around you . . .

Allow yourself to feel the pleasure that this beautiful day offers.

    Pause 15 seconds.

In the distance is a gray cloud . . .
and you notice that the wind is beginning to pick up . . .
Watch this distant cloud swirl and reach down to the earth . . .
the cloud is forming a tornado . . .

As you watch the tornado . . .
it grows and continues to grow until it reaches its full size . . .
This tornado draws upon all the energy that you have generated in
your life . . . every thought . . . every action . . . every dream . . .
and every emotion . . . and all the energy of your words . . .
written . . . spoken . . . and shouted . . .

    Pause 10 seconds.

Now, standing in the field, watch the tornado sweep toward you.

As you watch it grow in size and speed, you may feel some
apprehension . . . for you are not sure you will be safe from its
destructive force . . .

Observe this force as it collects all your possessions . . .
and everything you have experienced emotionally and physically . . .
jobs . . . fears . . . hopes . . . dreams . . . failures . . . successes.
All these elements feed the tornado and energize it . . .

    Pause 15 seconds.

TORNADO

Once the tornado has reached its full strength,
it halts before you in the center of the field . . .
It has swept up the physical and spiritual energy of your life,
and all it needs now is you . . .
You realize that the tornado is waiting for you to enter . . .

Walk now into your tornado
and feel yourself gently lifted into it . . .
You are carried upward, above the ground, with all the artifacts of
your life swirling around you . . .

The speed of the wind is tremendous, and you no longer can see the
bright day outside . . . When you look straight up through the
center, however, you see the calm blue sky.

 ↜ *Pause 10 seconds.*

The tornado builds and maintains even greater energy for the job it
must do . . . Although it is going to rearrange your life according to
your desires, you have no direct control over the tornado . . .

It is beyond you now . . . you are merely another piece of your
whole life, whirled in the tornado . . .
Watch the objects and interactions fly around you and realign.

Some pieces of your life are thrown out . . .
objects and concerns of no further use . . .
Some pieces rise . . .
because they are ready to change with you as you rise . . .
Others are too heavy, yet too valuable to discard . . . and they sink
from sight as you ride up the column of your tornado.

 ↜ *Pause 20 seconds.*

As you rise comfortably . . . you notice that the tornado spins
wherever you choose . . . wherever a problem exists . . .
at home, at school, at the office, or in any other place . . .
your tornado will carry you there and move the pieces around to
your satisfaction . . .

Whether it's a love situation in the present or past . . .
misunderstandings with friends or relatives . . . tasks you cannot
seem to finish . . . or problems with money . . . your tornado picks
them up and spins them around so the pieces can be set down in a
new combination . . .

allowing you to observe them from a different perspective.

꙳ *Pause 20 seconds.*

As the tornado picks up everything and spins it around . . .
you continue to rise calmly through the center . . .

Soon you will have risen to the top of your tornado.

꙳ *Pause 5 seconds.*

Now, at its peak, you look down upon the distant landscapes while
the energy of your life spirals beneath you . . .

Allow yourself to feel the triumph of being on top of everything
and knowing that everything is changing for the better . . .
or will be rearranged so that you may approach it with greater ease.

꙳ *Pause 10 seconds.*

Soon the tornado begins to travel to the places where it will set down
the pieces of your life . . .

The tornado deposits each item in its most suitable position . . .
The objects and activities that did not rise and change get cast off
first . . . and then the altered pieces find their niches.

꙳ *Pause 10 seconds.*

Finally the tornado lowers you gently down to the open field . . .
You watch it dwindle and fade on the wind . . .

Once again, you find yourself in a sunny pasture
on a warm, breezy day . . .
Outside all is calm . . .
Inside, feel yourself refreshed and collected . . .

Enjoy this good, renewed feeling . . .
as you slowly open your eyes once again to your familiar landscape.

GROUP PROCESSING OPTION

▨ Make some quick notes (perhaps in a journal) describing what
objects and activities were discarded, changed, and/or rearranged by
your tornado. Note your feelings about these changes and share them
with a partner (or small group).

Chapter 10

SCRIPTS *for* COPING

The empowering images in this chapter help participants develop
alternative strategies for dealing with stress, tension, emotional
pain, and illness.

Fall Colors

Imagine your feelings and attitudes changing
as the leaves turn color in the fall.

GOAL

To effectively cope with change.

TIME

4–5 minutes

MATERIALS

Large sheet of newsprint and markers (for Group Processing Option).

SPECIAL CONSIDERATIONS

Ideal for groups dealing with issues of change and life transitions.

GUIDED IMAGE SCRIPT

Begin by feeling the surface upon which your body is now resting . . . letting this surface totally support your body . . . and while your body gently gives way to a state of relaxation . . . let your eyelids become heavy . . . very heavy . . . until finally your eyes feel so heavy they must close.

Let your eyes close . . .
while you relax deeper and deeper
into the surface which supports you . . .
allowing your body to give way to total relaxation . . .

⸙ *Pause 5 seconds.*

In your mind, imagine a vivid color . . .
Focus on a color that brings you pleasure
and a sense of comfort . . .

Allow that comfort to enter and relax every aspect of yourself . . .
as you are filled with color.

Your special color washes through and over your body,
making you feel warm and relaxed . . .

    Pause 10 seconds.

As you continue to relax . . .
your breathing becomes slower . . .
and your body rests comfortably.

    Pause 10 seconds.

Imagine now a special, beautiful tree . . .
whose fall colors are especially vibrant . . .
A tree you return to year after year, because of its special colors . . .

Picture this tree . . .
and imagine its colors going through the seasons . . .

As the tree trades its green leaves for a dark red shade,
imagine your own feelings of tension doing the same . . .
changing color . . .
becoming cooler with the weather . . .

    Pause 15 seconds.

Now picture those red leaves changing to orange . . .
and from orange to bright yellow . . .

Imagine the light that those bright yellow leaves
throw on the ground beneath . . .

    Pause 10 seconds.

Now place your own mind in that transitional state . . .
shifting slowly from agitation to a peaceful relaxation . . .

    Pause 20 seconds.

Once you have made this transition
as much as you can at this time . . .
consider your image complete for now . . .

You may return to this colorful, relaxing image anytime you choose, but for now, it is now time to make the transition back to this room . . .

Once again, become aware of the surface upon which your body has been resting . . .

And become aware of your breathing, as well . . .

~ *Pause 10 seconds.*

As you listen to my voice,
it leads you back to a full state of awareness . . .
You will open your eyes . . .
and awaken from your experience.

~ *Pause 5 seconds.*

Now, open your eyes and awaken.

GROUP PROCESSING OPTION

▧ Reflect on times in your life that you had to "change your colors," i.e. change your mind, your attitudes, your feelings, and/or behaviors. What helped you to make these changes?

▧ Share with the entire group some of the things that helped to facilitate change.

~ *Record all ideas on large newsprint, identifying common themes.*

Resting Fish

*Regain mental buoyancy as you float
effortlessly with the fish.*

GOAL

To facilitate coping and acceptance.

To stay vibrant under stress.

TIME

2–3 minutes

SPECIAL CONSIDERATIONS

An easy, non-threatening exercise, appropriate for most groups.

GUIDED IMAGE SCRIPT

Sand, water, and warm weather . . .
a favorite setting to imagine resting . . . relaxing . . .
and closing your eyes . . .

Take the time to imagine resting and relaxing right now . . .
As you close your eyes . . .
imagine you are at the beach in a place of tropical beauty . . .

Pause 10 seconds.

You are on a sandy beach . . .
standing peacefully . . .
You breathe in deeply . . .
and exhale fully . . .

It is warm, and as you approach the water . . .
you see that it is calm, clear, and shallow . . .

You spot a small, colorful tropical fish in shallow water . . .
coming in to shore . . .
to rest where it is less turbulent . . .

Choosing a safe spot, this vibrant fish remains buoyant . . .

Watch the fins moving gently in the water . . .
keeping the fish at the same depth . . .
the fish appears unconscious of its efforts to remain buoyant . . .

    ↩ *Pause 10 seconds.*

Let this buoyancy linger in your mind
until you feel as though you are light and floating yourself . . .

    ↩ *Pause 10 seconds.*

Feeling light and buoyant . . .
allow this sensation to carry you back here . . .
to the present . . .
to this room . . .

    ↩ *Pause 10 seconds.*

And now . . . awaken . . .
and open your eyes.

GROUP PROCESSING OPTION

▧ Use the power of visualization to create in your imagination a special, ten-minute rest and refreshment break you can do for yourself. It should be something you can do easily today.

Take time to plan out details for what, how, where, when—then make a commitment to act on this plan sometime today.

▧ Share your plan with the group.

Spinal Elongation

Lie down and stretch your spine to alleviate accumulated tension.

GOAL

To help cope with the physical effects of stress.

TIME

3–4 minutes

SPECIAL CONSIDERATIONS

Participants will need to lie down on a hard flat surface such as a carpeted floor. It's best if people are wearing loose, comfortable clothing.

↭ *Demonstrate the stretching methods as you give verbal instructions.*

WARMUP

▨ Have you ever wondered why you often need to adjust the car mirror at the end of the work day? No one has been in the car since you left it parked and the mirror has not moved. You have shrunk!

▨ Your spine has reacted to stress and compressed. It is a sign of how your body was physically affected by the stress of the day.

▨ In fact, you are considerably taller in the morning than at the end of the day because your spine has had all night to decompress.

▨ This stretching technique is most effective when done in the afternoon or evening, when your spine is at its most compressed position.

GUIDED STRETCH SCRIPT

We'll begin by lying down, face up, on the floor . . .

Move your shoulders up and towards each other,
as if they might touch right in front of you . . .

At the same time, arch your back upward . . .
so that your spine curves away from the floor.

Your shoulder blades remain in contact with the ground
and you will feel the tension release gradually.

The stretch you may feel is taking place in your *rhomboid*
muscles . . . the long thin muscles located down both sides of your
upper spine.

Stretch only to the point of resistance . . . without straining . . .
then back off . . . to ensure a gentle relaxation.

Now, release the stretch . . .
gently lowering your spine and shoulders back to the floor.

Take a few moments to try this easy stretch on your own . . .
taking care not to strain . . . focusing on gentle relaxation . . .

⤺ Pause 60 seconds.

Notice how wonderful it feels to move . . . stretch . . .
awaken . . . and relax your body . . .

And when you are ready to go on with your day . . .
get up slowly and return to your place . . .
bringing your sense of calm and vitality with you.

GROUP PROCESSING OPTION

▨ Try this exercise at home, at the end of the work day, for a quick
release of stress and tension.

Sanctuary

Create a safe internal refuge where you can retreat to experience comfort, protection, and tranquillity.

GOAL

To reduce stress and facilitate coping.

TIME

6–8 minutes

SPECIAL CONSIDERATIONS

Adaptable for most groups. Particularly effective for people under severe stress.

Music playing quietly in the background enhances the impact of this visualization. Try Gregorian chants, non-melodic low-pitched *space* music, or *andante* movements from the classical tradition (cello, oboe, organ, symphonic). Burning incense adds atmosphere.

WARMUP

▒ At times we need to retreat to a safety zone, where we can get back in touch with ourselves and the world.

▒ Be designing your own sanctuary, you will have a permanent place to visit whenever you feel out of balance, overloaded, or unable to move forward, a place of refuge where you are not judged, criticized, or pressured, a place where you feel only relaxed and positive.

GUIDED IMAGE SCRIPT

Everyone needs a safety zone . . .
a place where you can temporarily retreat
when you are overwhelmed, worried or stuck . . .
a place where you can always feel positive and relaxed . . .
This *sanctuary* is only a daydream away . . .

To find your special retreat for today,
just settle back and exhale deeply a few times . . .

Let your breath rush out with a big whoosh or sigh . . .
and when you begin to feel relaxed, close your eyes . . .

Just let the music or your breathing lead you to your inner sanctuary.

෴ *Pause 15 seconds.*

To create your special retreat, recall places from your past
that gave you a sense of security and strength . . .
perhaps you remember a vacation spot . . .
or the home of relatives or friends . . .

Envision a tranquil place that felt comfortable . . .
and as you recall this place, become aware of all the details that gave
you intense pleasure and serenity . . .

෴ *Pause 20 seconds.*

Now, keeping the most pleasant aspects in mind,
revisit a favorite childhood haven . . .

This time recall a smaller, special space of your own . . .
it may be a treehouse . . . a hideout . . . a playroom . . .
or a private booth in the corner store.

Take sufficient time to recreate all the sensations . . .
smells . . .
noises . . .
shapes . . .
colors . . .
and textures
that allow you to relive those special memories.

෴ *Pause 20 seconds.*

Having re-experienced your feelings in these real places,
you are ready to create your ideal sanctuary . . .

Remember, once you create your sanctuary
you have total control over it . . .
Nothing will happen here without your permission . . .
You are free to tear up old floors . . .

open the place to the weather and the wind . . .
make things grow in whatever way you choose.

The only limitations are your own self-imposed boundaries.
Take some time now to create a sanctuary for yourself.

    Pause 15 seconds.

Now, explore your creation . . .
Look around and become aware of your surroundings . . .
Notice the quality of the light . . .
its brightness or subdued character . . .
Feel the light bathe over and into you . . .
washing every aspect of yourself.

    Pause 10 seconds.

What does your sanctuary look like?
Touch the floor and feel its texture and temperature . . .
Do the same for the walls and the other objects . . .

Feel free to change anything that does not feel comfortable . . .

You may become aware of certain objects or images
that represent the safety . . . security . . . tranquility . . .
beauty . . . and peace . . . that you cherish
in this place of refuge and relaxation . . .
familiar, comfortable aspects of yourself
that you wish to have in this sanctuary.

Focus your attention upon any of these special components of your
sanctuary . . .
Explore it using all your senses . . .
touch . . .
smell . . .
sight . . .
and sound . . .

Totally immerse yourself in it . . .
and allow yourself to enjoy the sensations and memories that it may
evoke . . .

    Pause 15 seconds.

When you are done . . . find a comfortable place to sit
that will enable you to absorb all of your sanctuary . . .
and feel its comfort . . . protection . . . and beauty . . .

Become even more aware of the entire setting . . .
a place that will grow and change from time to time
as you re-enter it.

Every time you return . . . you will leave behind all your
worries . . . stresses . . . concerns . . . and judgments . . .
Here you may relax and take time to indulge.

This is your special place . . .
a place where you may get back in touch with the best part of
yourself . . . any time you choose.

    ✍ *Pause 20 seconds.*

Now, knowing that you may return at any time . . .
you are ready to leave your sanctuary
and return to your present surroundings . . .

Remember to hold onto these pleasurable feelings
and bring them back with you.

Now, staying relaxed and content . . .
slowly tune back into your breathing . . .

As you hear the rhythmic flow of your breathing,
you are now ready to awaken and open your eyes
bringing back the peace and power of your sanctuary.

    ✍ *Pause 10 seconds.*

And now, awaken.

GROUP PROCESSING OPTION

▢ Pair up with another group member and describe your sanctuary.
Share important details about specific sensations associated with this
special place.

▢ Reverse roles, allowing the second person to talk about his or her
sanctuary.

Health

*Tap in to the healing power of your mind
to alleviate physical discomfort or illness.*

GOAL
To promote self-healing.

TIME
8–10 minutes

SPECIAL CONSIDERATIONS
Most appropriate for groups whose stated goal is some form of
healing. Since participants lie down during the visualization, cots,
exercise mats, or comfortable carpeting is essential.

WARMUP
Throughout history, imagery has been related to healing. Some
societies drew pictures to represent illness and vanquished it through
song or chants. Others had the shaman or medicine man perform
rituals that conquered the disease.

These same principles are still being used today. At the forefront of
cancer research, patients use mental imagery to combat terminal
illness. Patients construct pictures of the strong and the infected
portions of their bodies. They surround the infected areas with the
healthy parts and fight them one by one.

These simple methods direct the person's attention to the body and
its health.

Many health problems today are attributed to stress that inhibits
the body's powers of healing.

If given the opportunity, the body has the ability to heal itself of
many ailments. When bruised, attacked by a virus, or not sufficiently
rested, a person may relax, focus attention upon the neglected or
injured areas, and give the body a chance to do its work.

In this guided image, you are going to practice healing an area of your body. Once familiar with the technique, you may use it to alleviate the discomfort of many ailments, illnesses, or disease.

⇝ *This visualization works best when participants are lying down with legs uncrossed and hands at their sides.*

GUIDED IMAGE SCRIPT

Begin by breathing slowly and deeply . . .
focusing your attention on the surface of your entire body . . .

Slowly inhale and exhale a few times . . .
You are relaxing your body . . .
and as you become aware of your breathing . . .
you focus on the surface of your body.

⇝ *Pause 15 seconds.*

As you drift deeper into a state of relaxation,
prepare to take a journey within your own body . . .

You are going to journey through the interior of your body,
taking note of its operations
and assessing any areas where trouble exists . . .

In order to make this journey,
close your eyes and imagine your body resting on the bed . . .

As you picture your body,
imagine a perfectly healthy image emerging from it . . .

This image approximates your body in size and shape . . .
When the image of your body emerges completely
it begins to shrink, becoming denser, miniature, compact . . .
Your spirit self has shrunk to a tiny replica of your physical self . . .
and you find yourself looking out through the eyes of this
miniature . . . at the seemingly enormous body before you . . .

You are ready to begin your journey.

Finding an entryway . . .
through mouth, ear, nostril, or skin pore . . .
you slip into the massive, resting body lying on the bed . . .

Once inside your body,
you will find yourself traveling through the blood vessels . . .
These vessels are like hallways . . . or corridors . . .
which crisscross the living tissues . . .

↩ *Pause 10 seconds.*

As you travel through the arteries, veins, and capillaries . . .
note the appearance of all the healthy portions of your body.

You will find stringy, striped bands of muscles . . .

↩ *Pause 10 seconds.*

Curving white bones providing the superstructure and separating the
various organs . . .

↩ *Pause 10 seconds.*

The heart squeezing and relaxing itself . . .

↩ *Pause 10 seconds.*

The stomach breaking down food and forwarding it to other places
for further processing . . .

↩ *Pause 10 seconds.*

The liver carrying on its complex chemical industries . . .

↩ *Pause 10 seconds.*

The brain transmitting electrical impulses to all regions,
like a humming power plant . . .

↩ *Pause 10 seconds.*

Visit all the other parts of your body to inspect their operation . . .

↩ *Pause 20 seconds.*

On your inspection, you will pass white corpuscles . . .
these are the antibodies, the body's soldiers that seek out and destroy
any intruders in their sector . . .
Unfortunately, they have been operating for years with no specific
direction, only the general objective . . .
to protect the body by destroying any intruders in their sector . . .

The white blood cells recognize that you are friendly . . .

As you pass among them . . .
you notice a particular region where a battle is going on . . .

As an onlooker, you notice the disorganization and realize that the
corpuscles must have a leader to win . . .
You listen to strategic reports about the invaders' stronghold and
begin to marshal the troops . . .

You visualize a plan of attack and inform your troops that there can
be no surrender if this foe is to be forever vanquished . . .

All your troops are restless with anticipation . . .
They rally to your call, and other white cells from neighboring
sectors leave their routine patrols to aid their comrades in battle . . .

As the troops gain in strength, the attack is launched . . .
Several of the largest white cells rush in and begin to engulf invader
cells . . . Other corpuscles attack the intruder's flank and isolate
enemy cells from the rest of their forces . . .

Continuing your assault, you watch the weakened enemy retreat
back to another sector, but your victory is not yet complete . . .
While the enemy retreats . . . you watch some of your troops being
carried off the battlefield and know you will need reinforcements to
have a total victory.

You must attack and finish the fight . . . so you dispatch orders for
more white cells to be sent from the bone marrow factories where
they are manufactured and stand ready . . .

As your remaining troops continue to pursue, the reinforcements
sweep in from the blood vessels . . .
Together, they overwhelm and crush the enemy . . .

You have won the battle!

Once you have destroyed the enemy within . . . tell your troops that
you will revisit them any time leadership is needed . . .
All they need is to send a message to your brain, and you will come
to their aid.

You bid your troops good-bye
and thank them all for a job well done . . .

You begin your journey back through the body along the path by which you came . . . back to the point of your initial entry . . .

↫ *Pause 15 seconds.*

When you have arrived at this place, your tiny self exits . . .
Once outside the body, you begin to expand into a mist-like replica of your physical body . . .

As soon as you reach full size,
you begin to reconnect with your physical body . . .

As you complete the connection . . .
become aware of your breathing . . .
and consciously bring your rate of breathing to a waking state . . .

↫ *Pause 10 seconds.*

Now, count to three . . .
and as you exhale, you awaken . . .
refreshed and relaxed.

GROUP PROCESSING OPTIONS

▨ Draw an outline of your body, then mark the places you visited in your journey. Use a different symbol to mark areas of your body you wanted to explore, but did not.

▨ Jot down some notes about one of your current health concerns and your thoughts about how this kind of visualization might impact your well-being. Share your drawing and your insights with your small group.

HOMEWORK

▨ Memorize the image of your healthy spirit self. Practice inviting your spirit into your body whenever you want help in fighting off illness.

Superpowers

Activate imaginary magic powers to cope with feelings of helplessness and for making changes you never thought possible.

GOAL

To facilitate coping and healing.

TIME

8–10 minutes

SPECIAL CONSIDERATIONS

Ideal for workshops and groups focused on family of origin issues. Probably not appropriate for worksite. Could elicit old, painful memories from childhood.

Using a lighted candle as a focal point can greatly enhance this image, but is probably risky in most group settings.

WARMUP

When we were children, we all fantasized about having superpowers that would enable us to transcend our relatively power-less state. Magic powers would make us instantly equal to the adults who towered over us and seemed to run everything.

In fact, we would become more than adults. Perhaps with the help of comic heroes like Superman, Wonder Woman, Captain Marvel, the Flash, or Spiderman, we imagined ourselves saving the world, capturing villains, and instantly cleaning up our room.

Such fantasies project a world we would want if we had the power to change it. If we recreate our dream of superpowers and enter into it today, we can learn more about our relationship to and attitudes toward the world as it is.

■ This image creates situations that you must live out on your own. There will be long pauses in the guided imagery where you will be expected to explore your fantasy on your own before continuing.

GUIDED IMAGE SCRIPT

↪ *Be sure to allow plenty of time for participants to "live out" their images in the visualization.*

Sit back and relax now, as you prepare for a surge of magical power . . .

Imagine that you are gazing at a lighted candle, set before you on a table . . .

Allow your gaze to focus on the flame . . .
burning steady and bright . . .
and as you watch the shape and motion of the flame,
allow your mind to dwell on the flame
as the symbol of eternal life and rebirth . . .

Think of the Phoenix . . .
a bird consumed in flame only to rise again from its ashes . . .

Still focusing on the flame . . .
if thoughts or images stray into your mind, just allow them to pass through and move on . . .
as you continue to focus on the flame and your steady breathing.

↪ *Pause 10 seconds.*

As you become more and more relaxed,
allow your mind to drift back into childhood,
when you were so much smaller . . .

Recall how adults seemed capable of things you couldn't do . . .
They seemed larger then and had access to places you were not allowed to go . . .

While brooding on this inequality . . .
you walk the streets of your childhood neighborhood . . .
Suddenly you come to a side street you haven't seen before . . .
and spot a darkened curio shop.

When you peek inside the window, a kindly-looking old man with small round glasses and white hair looks up and beckons to you . . .
He smiles, and as you step inside the shop you hear him say . . .
"Come in, come in, I've been waiting for you!"

You barely have time to glimpse the beautiful old books . . .
the musty cloaks . . .
the bottles of colored liquid . . .
and many other wonders that line the aisles . . .
as he takes you by the hand to the back of the shop . . .
"I have just the item you need!" he says excitedly . . .

As you watch curiously,
he opens a small drawer and pulls out a golden ring . . .
it catches the light and sparkles . . .
He holds it up and says . . .
"This ring belonged to Merlin, who never used it.
It gives the wearer whatever magical power he or she desires . . ."

"As you put on the ring, you must say out loud the power you wish to possess . . . and you shall have it . . ."

"But it only works as long as you wear the ring . . .
the minute you take it off, your power is gone, never to return."

You begin to think of your helplessness, and the things you *could* do if you had superpowers . . .

Perhaps you recall the heroines and heroes in your comic books . . .
and remember how you longed to possess their powers of
X-ray vision . . . amazing speed . . . astounding strength . . .
invisibility . . . certainty . . . and more . . .

Or perhaps you have longed for magical powers because you keep running into a problem or situation that some magic capability would help you resolve with ease . . .

But which power do you want the most? . . .
The old man in the curio shop waits patiently. . . .

You must choose.

↩ *Pause 5 seconds.*

Once you have made your choice,
you smile and he hands you the ring.

You name your chosen superpower out loud
and slip on the ring . . .
In an instant you find yourself empowered with that special
something else that you have desired.

The curio shop owner waves good-bye as you step out of the
shop . . . eager to test your new capability . . .

Standing on the sidewalk a moment,
you think about what you are going to do first . . .
You want to exercise your new power in some way that will benefit
you and perhaps other people as well . . .
What will it be?

You ponder and then decide . . .

∽ *Pause 10 seconds.*

Now you are doing it . . .
using your superpower just as you want to.

Notice how it feels to exercise your power in this way . . .
and notice the effects of your action.

Once you have completed this first deed,
two or three others occur to you . . .
Allow yourself to perform each one in turn . . .
paying particular attention to your feelings as you do them.

∽ *Pause 20 seconds.*

Now that you've had a chance to exert your magical powers
in several ways . . .
allow yourself to pause and take stock of the situation . . .

What would it mean to live the rest of your life with this
power? . . .
Do you feel that it poses any new obligations? . . .
How will your new status affect your relations with family and
friends?

∽ *Pause 10 seconds.*

You have to decide whether you wish to keep this potent capability for the rest of your life . . .

If you do, what use do you expect to make of it in the future? . . . If not, why not?

↩ *Pause 10 seconds.*

Now that you've exercised your superpower in a number of situations, it's time to rest and reflect on the activities of this day . . .

You sit down, or lie down . . .
and think about all you've accomplished.

As you relax . . .
you feel your mind going deeper and deeper into a restful state.

When you are fully rested,
you will return to a state of full consciousness . . .
Ready to incorporate the insights from this healing vision . . .
into the challenges of your current life situations.

↩ *Pause 10 seconds.*

Allow yourself to return to full consciousness . . .
relaxed and energized.

GROUP PROCESSING OPTION

Pair up with another group member and share what power you picked, and why you desired this power as a child. Talk about how you used your new power and how you think it changed your relationships with people.

Then reverse roles so the other person can share his or her experiences.

Anger

Explore the sources of anger in your life as you mentally "blow off steam" and seek advice from a caring consultant.

GOAL

To increase self-awareness.

To promote positive anger management.

TIME

14–15 minutes

SPECIAL CONSIDERATIONS

This is a complex, difficult visualization which requires self-esteem and a willingness to risk vulnerability in order to change perceptions, attitudes, and behavior. Appropriate for assertiveness training, parenting classes, anger management training, or growth groups.

WARMUP

Sometimes we cannot express the source of our anger; we explode over trifles that have little or nothing to do with the real causes. Everyone needs a safe method of blowing off steam.

In this exercise you will have a chance to express anger you may be harboring, and perhaps identify its hidden sources.

GUIDED IMAGE SCRIPT

Prepare for this guided image by shaking out your body to relieve any muscle tension.
Shake your hands . . . and arms . . . shoulders . . . and head . . . feet . . . ankles . . . legs . . . butt . . . and torso . . .
Let all the tension that has accumulated anywhere in your body shake itself out . . .

⁀ *Pause 10 seconds.*

Now, settle into a comfortable position, close your eyes,
and allow yourself to relax even further . . .
breathing easily and deeply . . .
becoming more and more relaxed.

You are relaxing,
quieting yourself with the steady rhythm of your breathing . . .

⤺ *Pause 15 seconds.*

You are totally relaxed . . . and ready to explore your inner being.
Start by taking an inventory of your recent interactions . . .
Mentally go back through the incidents of the past few days . . .
and note any times when you felt put upon . . .
compromised . . . or violated in any way . . .

⤺ *Pause 10 seconds.*

Choose one such incident to focus on.
Notice any anger you may have felt as a result of this
experience . . .
What specifically triggered your anger? . . .
Replay this incident in your mind . . .
Pay close attention to all the details . . . where it was . . .
who was involved . . . and what happened.
Allow yourself to feel whatever you felt then . . .
re-experience your emotions . . .

⤺ *Pause 15 seconds.*

Now take a moment to release that memory and emotion . . .
Take a deep breath, and let your mind go blank . . .

⤺ *Pause 15 seconds.*

Now you are going to view this same incident again.
This time you are going to watch the incident from outside . . .
you will look at yourself being angry . . .

Observe the outward manifestations of your emotion . . .
what you say . . . how you say it . . .
what movements you make . . .
Notice what you appear like when you explode or become tense . . .

⤺ *Pause 15 seconds.*

Now examine the supposed cause of your anger . . .
Do the emotions and excitement seem to be appropriate to the situation?

   ↬ Pause 15 seconds.

Often we experience angry emotions that are more intense than what the situation objectively warrants . . .
so you should not be surprised if the magnitude of your rage seems too large for the incident.

There are several possible reasons for the extent of your anger . . .

You might have been angry about something else and just happened to explode at this moment over an unrelated issue . . .

Perhaps this current incident contained certain elements that your memory associated with important events in your past . . .
events that touched upon deeper sources of fear and insecurity . . .

In the heat of the moment, you may have been reacting to very old and deeply rooted concerns.

Now re-enter yourself and relive this recent incident . . .
As the event plays itself out . . . pay careful attention to the actions or words that seem to arouse you most . . . and the elements that seem to compromise or threaten you the most . . .

Do you feel misunderstood? . . . violated? . . . abandoned?

   ↬ Pause 20 seconds.

If nothing strikes a chord,
go back one more time and re-experience the angry scene . . .

   ↬ Pause 15 seconds.

If again nothing comes to the surface, you may have to acknowledge that this visualization is not working for you for this issue . . .
In that case, you may drop out of the exercise gracefully.
Just continue breathing and relaxing as you let the words drift through your mind.

If you did identify some deeper issues as you explored your anger, you are ready to re-enter the scene and make some adjustments.

Imagine yourself back at the beginning of the incident . . .

Allow yourself to feel the true emotions
and understand the real issues . . .

⌐ Pause 10 seconds.

You have reached the seat of the fire,
deep and hot without the blinding smoke . . .
After experiencing this understanding . . .
you are ready to conduct yourself with more restraint . . .

Replay the scene again.
This time do what is necessary to straighten things out . . .
If another person is involved,
ask that person any questions for which you need answers . . .
let the other person know exactly how you feel and what other issues
the incident brought up between you.

⌐ Pause 20 seconds.

Now it's time to search for other anger generators in your life.
This time, instead of reliving an incident in which you
exploded . . . you are going to identify an anger-producing issue you
have been silently carrying around.

We all have experiences we are unable to discard immediately from
our minds . . .
Perhaps you can identify one easily . . .
and perhaps you do not know what has been bothering you . . .
It could even be the case that something has been causing you to
build up anger
but you were too preoccupied to notice the tension . . .
Focus on one of these silent anger generators . . .

⌐ Pause 10 seconds.

Think of someone to whom you can vent your feelings . . .
not the source of your anger, but another person . . .
A friend . . . a partner . . . a mentor . . . or a therapist . . .
This person is safe because you are not angry with him or her . . .
you also know you can trust this person to listen patiently.

Imagine this caring confidant is joining you in your mental living
room.

As soon as the two of you are ready . . . begin to express your anger
as if you were in a provoking situation . . .
Allow yourself to observe the upsetting incidents . . .
Feel the anger build inside and surface . . .
Feel yourself acting on your emotion . . .

✍ *Pause 10 seconds.*

Once you have openly released your anger
and begun to calm down . . .
ask the person you have confided in to assess the situation . . .
Perhaps that person fully approves of the course you have taken . . .
Perhaps that person, while not disapproving, is a little surprised by
the force of your anger . . .
If so, the two of you must look at the situation together . . .

As in the first part of this exercise, step outside of the angry scene
and watch yourself in action . . .
Look at the provoking circumstances and your resulting fury . . .
if they do not seem to correspond then you must search for the true
source . . .

Take all the time you need to find it . . .
Perhaps your confidant will have suggestions.

✍ *Pause 30 seconds.*

It is time for you to finish your thoughts for the moment . . .
In a few seconds, it is time for you to awaken and return . . .

Now . . . awaken.

GROUP PROCESSING OPTION

▪ Pick one of the two incidents you remembered in the visualizations. Reflect on what you wanted from the other person in the
situation. Did this get communicated?

▪ Role-play this with a partner and practice saying what you
wanted, clearly and directly. Work on communicating respect for
yourself and the other person, then allow the other person to role-
play his or her situation.

Chapter 11

SCRIPTS *for* CONNECTEDNESS

The expansive images in this chapter stimulate reflection on our deep connections to other people, with nature, and with the wider world. Participants explore the physical, mental, and spiritual nourishment of relationships past, present, and future.

Rubber Band

Integrate your mind and body while letting go of tension in this quick stretch.

GOAL

To facilitate mind-body integration.

TIME

3-5 minutes

SPECIAL CONSIDERATIONS

Participants should arrange their chairs to have enough space around them for stretching their arms out to the side and overhead without bumping into another person.

This visualization and quick stretch could be used several times in the same session, adding more imagery and additional body stretches with each use.

WARMUP

The physical act of stretching is an essential part of any relaxation program. This exercise uses the power of the mind to enhance the physical act of stretching—a method of mind-body integration.

GUIDED IMAGE SCRIPT

Allow yourself to relax as much as possible in your chair . . . with your hands resting comfortably in your lap.

Uncross your legs and let your feet be flat on the floor . . .

Unbuckle your belt if if constricts your breathing . . .

↩ *Pause a moment, if necessary, while participants get comfortable and settled in their chairs.*

Take in a deep breath . . .
and as you exhale . . . let your eyes close.

With your eyes closed . . . continue to take slow, deep, easy breaths.

Give yourself permission to breathe with the full capacity of your lungs, at the same time letting your breathing be very relaxed . . . relaxed as a sleeping baby.

      ↪ *Pause 10 seconds.*

Now, keeping your back straight and uplifted,
continue to breathe deeply . . .
and slowly raise your arms out to your sides . . . in a giant arc . . .
stretch them upward to the sky . . .

Elongate your arms . . . and feel the stretch all the way from your lower back . . . through your arms . . . up your neck . . .
and to the end of your fingertips . . .

When you are ready . . .
simply lower your arms back to your sides . . . slowly . . .
and rest your hands comfortably in your lap.

      ↪ *Pause until participants are done stretching.*

With your eyes still closed . . . visualize pulling a rubber band until it is stretched taut . . .
then gently letting it go back to its orginal relaxed state.

This is similar to what is happening to your muscles when you stretch them.

You are going to stretch your arms again,
but this time you will concentrate on your muscles . . .
Do not pay attention to your arms . . .
but to the muscles inside your arms . . .
they are being pulled in two directions at once . . .
their fibers are being slightly separated . . .
and the increased blood flow in the muscles removes soreness and helps you relax.

Now, go ahead and start stretching your arms overhead again,
at your own pace . . .

Visualize the muscles inside your arms being pulled in two directions at once . . . the fibers being slightly separated . . .

the increased blood flow removing any soreness or tension you might hold in your arms . . . and helping you to relax . . .

Hold the stretch as long as you want . . .
then lower your arms and bring your hands back to your lap.

    ↩ *Pause until stretching is complete.*

Now, picture yourself in a different environment,
no longer sitting in this room . . .

How about on a giant wooden deck in the mountains,
or on a cliff above the ocean? . . .

It can be anywhere you choose.

Find your special place.

    ↩ *Pause 10 seconds.*

You will stretch your arms one last time . . .

While you imagine sitting or standing in your special relaxing place,
stretch your arms overhead . . . reaching to the sky . . .
Visualize the muscles inside your arms
being pulled in two directions at once . . .
the fibers being slightly separated . . .
as you take in this special place around you . . .
the increased blood flow removing any soreness or tension lurking in your arms . . .

You are totally relaxed . . .
Hold this stretch as long as you want . . .
breathing deeply . . .
until you are ready to bring your arms back down to your sides comfortably.

You have completed this stretch for now . . .
Notice how you feel when you are done.

GROUP PROCESSING OPTION

▨ Talk with others in your small group about your stretching experience. What images or feelings surfaced for you?

Dew off a Leaf

Reconnect with creation as you observe the ripple effects of a dew drop falling in the lake.

GOAL

To connect with the calming aspect of nature.

TIME

2–3 minutes

SPECIAL CONSIDERATIONS

Appropriate for use in a broad variety of group settings, including wilderness groups, spiritual retreats, support groups, etc.

Helpful to use quiet music in the background. A solo piano, harp, or guitar would fit the simple imagery.

GUIDED IMAGE SCRIPT

Let your mind wander and drift now to thoughts of buoyancy . . . floating . . . drifting . . . and relaxing . . .

Simply close your eyes and listen to the words I speak . . . As you listen, allow yourself to relax.

↩ *Read the list of words slowly.*

Comfort . . . release . . . coast . . . ease . . . open . . . mellow out . . . loose . . . tranquil . . . refresh . . . bask . . . slacken . . . free . . . revitalize . . . enjoy . . . delight . . . diminish . . . peaceful . . . savor . . . loaf . . . taper off . . . free thoughts . . . siesta . . . rest . . . lessen . . . energize . . . soften . . . unwind . . . unbend . . . carefree . . . pause . . . at ease . . . breathe easy . . . float . . . wane . . . recline . . . serene . . . repose . . . lie down . . . feathery . . . take your time . . . relief . . . and relax.

Now imagine at this moment
that you are sitting on the shore of a protected lake . . .
it is very peaceful and calm . . .
and the water is a deep blue . . .

The lake is surrounded by trees . . .
the trees have full, green leaves hanging from their branches . . .

Imagine a single drop of dew resting on a leaf . . .
the leaf is on a tree which hangs over an expanse of flat,
undisturbed water . . .

As the dew rolls down the leaf . . .
feel tension giving way to gravity . . .
gradually releasing hold of the leaf . . .
then falling slowly toward the water . . .

As the dewdrop is welcomed into the water,
imagine the ripples it creates . . .
Each enlarges slowly and gradually . . .
This continues as its action is absorbed by the lake . . .

Soon the lake is back to a relaxed, undisturbed,
and smooth state once again . . .

It is no longer a single falling drop . . .
you are now part of a large breadth of calm, soothing water.

Having become a part of this larger body of water . . .
as you consciously tune back into your surroundings
and my voice . . .
it is now time to rejoin us and awaken.

GROUP PROCESSING OPTION

Recall a time when you felt deeply connected to nature. What are
the images and other sensory memories connected to this experience?
Share your responses with the group.

Discuss ways that people in the group maintain and nourish these
connections with nature.

Satisfying Your Thirst

Discover the whole person nourishing power of
nature on a quiet stroll by a crystal stream.

GOAL

To feel revitalized in body, mind, and spirit.

TIME

2–3 minutes

GUIDED IMAGE SCRIPT

In preparation for this journey,
take a deep breath and close your eyes . . .

As you inhale, roll your eyes upwards,
behind your closed lids . . .
then as you exhale,
let your eyes relax and rest wherever is comfortable . . .

Your eyes are relaxed . . .
your lids are heavy . . .
and any tension you might be carrying in your forehead is dissolving
away . . .

You are floating gently and continually into a state of relaxation.

As you continue to relax,
imagine that you are hiking in a remote wooded area,
far from any roads, towns, or people . . .

　Pause 10 seconds.

You come across a crystal clear stream of water . . .

It appears as though no one has ever been in this part of the
woods . . . and the stream is completely pure and natural . . .

You are in a state of awe.

Thirsty from your travels . . .
you kneel down along the mossy shoreline to drink . . .

Taste how crisp and fresh this water is . . .
feel it entering into your body . . .

As it is absorbed within you . . .
every cell in your body is revitalized.

⤳ *Pause 15 seconds.*

This sensation is an experience to be shared . . .

Bring it back with you now as you open your eyes . . .
and return from your journey

GROUP PROCESSING OPTION

▨ If this visualization were a metaphor for non-physical needs (spiritual, emotional, mental, or social) what would you be thirsting for? Jot your responses in a column on a sheet of paper or in your journal.

▨ What actions can you take to satisfy this thirst? For each non-physical thirst you listed, make note of at least one action you could take to satisfy that thirst.

▨ Share some or all of your responses with a partner.

Music

Get in touch with yourself—
body, mind, spirit, and emotions —
as you tune in to the music of life.

GOAL

To relax and refresh through music.

TIME

5–6 minutes

MATERIALS NEEDED

Portable stereo and musical selections featuring at least three instruments (e.g., Modern Jazz quartet, Big Band sound, Calypso group, symphony, string quartet, marching band).

For Variation: cassette player with headphones for each participant. Extra batteries. Broad selection of taped music featuring at least three instruments (see above). Be sure to have enough cassettes so every participant has a wide choice for private listening.

SPECIAL CONSIDERATIONS

The maximum benefit of this visualization will come when individuals listen to their own choice of music, at their own pace, as suggested in the Variation. But any group will appreciate the communal experience, as well. An excellent warmup for a team-building discussion on interdependence.

WARMUP

▧ One common way to relax is to listen to music. Teenagers rank this activity as their number one choice for stress management.

▧ In this guided image, you will be invited not only to hear music, but to become totally immersed within it.

▧ After listening and relaxing to the music for a short time, you will close your eyes and focus your attention on the music. As you become involved in the music, you may feel and see the musical notes flowing from their sources.

↪ *Start the music softly, then increase the volume until the music is loud enough to feel the vibrations.*

GUIDED IMAGE SCRIPT

Allow yourself to get comfortable and relaxed . . . gradually tuning out the world around you as you tune into the music.
Close your eyes . . . and let the rhythm of your breathing follow the steady beat of the music.

As you focus on the sound . . .
begin to feel it filling the room and enveloping you . . .
Feel your body respond to vibrations in the music . . .

↪ *Pause 10 seconds. Music should be loud enough to vibrate, but not so loud as to harm hearing.*

Notice which parts of you feel the vibrations . . .
and allow that feeling to spread throughout your body . . .
gradually feel yourself becoming in tune with the music . . .

As you hear and feel each note . . .
you may notice various instruments . . .
appearing either individually or as part of an entire ensemble . . .

Allow each instrument to appear.

Gradually . . .
you will hear one instrument grow distinct from the others . . .
focus your attention on this instrument . . .
You may picture the instrument itself . . .
yourself playing the instrument . . .
or you may even imagine yourself becoming the instrument . . .

↪ *Pause 10 seconds.*

Notice the way the air vibrates . . .
inside and around this instrument . . .
the air moving in waves.

↪ *Pause 10 seconds.*

Imagine what sort of aroma would accompany the sounds this instrument is making . . . and allow yourself to smell it . . .

⤾ *Pause 10 seconds.*

Visualize a string of the notes dancing together . . .
perhaps you will dance with them.

⤾ *Pause 10 seconds.*

Gradually your concentration on this instrument fades . . .
and you begin to distinguish another instrument . . .
Focus your attention on this new instrument . . .

⤾ *Pause 10 seconds.*

Feel the way fingers press, beat, caress, or pluck at the instrument . . .
Perhaps the instrument is under your fingers . . . or perhaps you are the instrument and someone else's fingers play you . . .

⤾ *Pause 10 seconds.*

Again, feel the air vibrate around and within the instrument . . .
experience the sounds and sensations of every note . . .
Allow yourself to feel each note . . . touch it . . . and smell it, if you can.

⤾ *Pause 10 seconds.*

Eventually, you hear a third instrument
separate from the other sounds . . .
Focus your attention on the sound of this instrument . . .
hearing and feeling each note . . .

⤾ *Pause 10 seconds.*

As you listen, this instrument may appear . . .
You may see yourself playing this instrument . . .
or perhaps you are being played . . .
See . . . hear . . . and feel this instrument completely.

⤾ *Pause 10 seconds.*

Now the instruments re-integrate as total musical sound . . .
Allow yourself to hear and feel all the instruments
blending together . . .

MUSIC

207

You may begin to feel the vibrations spreading rhythmically
throughout your body . . .
Allow the music to completely fill your body . . .

   ↩ *Pause 10 seconds.*

You may picture a group of instruments or musicians . . .
or you may imagine that you are the orchestra or band . . .
Allow yourself to hear . . . feel . . . and see the music fully . . .
Slowly blend with the music, and feel it becoming one with you.

Eventually, you will sense the music coming to an end . . .
As the notes subside . . . the vibrations in your body decrease . . .

Your images will begin to fade as the notes diminish . . .
allow the notes to dissipate . . .

When all the notes have departed . . .
focus on the stillness . . . listen to the silence . . .
allow yourself to feel the lack of motion in your body . . .

   ↩ *Slowly turn off the music and then pause 10 seconds.*

Relax in the stillness for a few moments . . .
and when you are ready . . . open your eyes.

GROUP PROCESSING OPTION

▓ Introduce yourself to the group by completing the sentence,
"If I were a musical instrument, I would be a . . . "

▓ Take a few minutes to explain your choice.

VARIATION

▓ Distribute headphone cassette players and invite participants to
repeat the process, using music of their choice from your selection.
Set a time limit, then keep time for the group, announcing when
there is about a minute left. You may want to outline the steps of the
process on newsprint for easy reference.

▓ Remind participants that when they are doing this at home, they
need to select a piece of music in which they can distinguish at least
three instruments.

Chain Reaction

Discover how even the smallest actions can have powerful impacts on the people in your life.

GOAL

To develop skills for making positive connections with people.

TIME

12–15 minutes

SPECIAL CONSIDERATIONS

Ideal for work-site team-building, communication, or assertiveness groups.

WARMUP

When we try to evaluate how well we have fared during the day, over the past week, or throughout the year, we typically focus on the major events—the big accomplishments, the major battles, or the most painful defeats.

Most of us don't consider the power that *all* of our actions have, even small ones, such as honking at a stranger or saying a simple, "Hello, you look nice today."

Every action counts. We don't think much of the minor ones because their effects seem so small, but cumulatively they can have as great an impact as the major ones.

In this exercise, you are going to focus on a couple of small interactions from the last day or two and follow their impact on another person's life. You may discover that your every move, no matter how small, adds something to the lives of others—in potentially both negative and positive ways.

GUIDED IMAGE SCRIPT

Make yourself comfortable,
and spend a few minutes tuning into your body . . .

Allow your body to feel light as a feather or a cloud . . .
Feeling empty and free as you close your eyes . . .

With your eyes closed, take a few slow deep breaths . . .
and allow yourself to relax . . . letting the tension drain out of your
body with every exhaling breath . . .

You may feel this relaxation developing and expanding as you
continue to breathe deeply . . .

⤷ *Pause 15 seconds.*

As you continue to relax comfortably, mentally go back over the
interactions you had with people yesterday . . .

You are going to identify a minor negative interaction with a
stranger . . . something on the order of honking your horn, cutting
in front of someone, or speaking rudely to someone . . .

Mentally recall your day . . . and choose one relatively minor negative interaction for your focus.

⤷ *Pause 10 seconds.*

Once you have identified such an exchange, play through the detail
of the scene in your mind . . . leaving all motivations aside . . .

Focus on the tone that your action set . . . and pinpoint whatever
changes occurred as a result of your behavior . . .
Recall any reaction as the stranger took in your message.

It is possible that the other person did not consciously register your
negative message . . . or did not take it in deeply . . .

Imagine that the person's face tenses just slightly into a scowl . . .
As co-workers notice that face, they register the message that the
person is not in the best mood . . .

Perhaps they may decide not to approach with problems . . .
perhaps they also warn other employees to tread lightly.

Meanwhile, the negative feeling percolates in the person

with whom you had a negative interaction . . .
It does not eat away at the individual's insides . . . but it does irritate
slightly . . . like a fly buzzing at the far end of the room . . .

This irritation makes the person less inclined to be gracious and
understanding with others.

Everyone seems to *want* things . . . and finally the person snaps . . .
shouting at another innocent someone to get out of the way . . .

This person, feeling hurt and defensive . . .
sends an employee on a meaningless errand . . .
and the employee runs into someone else in his haste . . .

In this way . . . ten, fifteen, or twenty people might be adversely
affected by the negative thing you did to the stranger you met . . .

   Pause 10 seconds.

Once you have gotten a sense of such a chain reaction,
you are ready to experience it through someone you know well . . .

Go back through yesterday's events again . . . and pick a negative
interaction you had with someone close to you . . .
Again it should be a minor event . . .
perhaps words spoken with impatience or ill-timed humor . . .

   Pause 10 seconds.

Now that you have chosen the event . . .
play it carefully through your memory . . .
However, this time, put yourself in the place of that close
acquaintance . . .

As the moment unfolds . . . you see the other person . . .
who was really you . . . hit you with a negative reaction
when you had expected something else . . .

Allow yourself to feel the confusion and hurt . . .

   Pause 5 seconds.

Suddenly you are not in a mood to waste time with other people's
petty concerns . . .
They don't appreciate all the work you have to do . . .
and they expect you to pick up after them when they haven't done

their homework . . .
and you just don't feel like doing it today . . .

A co-worker comes to you
and asks you to look at a problem with her . . .
"I'm all tied up today," you say calmly but with firmness . . .
"You will have to deal with it yourself . . . "

Your colleague turns away, puzzled,
carrying on a mental dialogue with you . . .
"Usually you're congenial," she tells you in her mind.

Even though she knows your rebuff was not a personal slight . . .
since it really had nothing to do with her request . . .
she can't help being annoyed . . . and she mentally tells you off:
"You could have made the effort to be courteous and helpful . . .
despite whatever was on your mind."

While your co-worker is brooding over this . . .
a maintenance man who is repairing the photocopy machine asks her
for a cigarette . . .
"No, I don't smoke," she says, with an intonation that suggests
contempt for anyone who does . . .

This unfriendly gesture irritates the repairman and sets off his guilt
about being unable to quit . . .
He passes on his annoyance to several other people . . .
who frown and snap at their clients . . .
and those clients carry their feelings to other offices . . .

Thus, your one negative act spreads like a small plague
and puts a crimp in the day for many people.

    Pause 10 seconds.

Now, let's revisit the scene.

Still in the role of your friend . . .
imagine returning to the person who started this chain
reaction . . . who was, of course, actually you . . .

Make yourself sit up and take notice of your friend's hurt . . .
then see yourself understand and apologize for the slight . . .

Next, imagine the female co-worker asking what had been on your

mind when you refused to assist her . . .
Listen to her explain how your refusal threw off her momentum
and caused her to snap at the repairman . . .

Once all of you have faced your part in the chain of unnecessary
negative interactions, you feel better.

   ↪ *Pause 5 seconds.*

Now that you have seen
how a chain of negative events can snowball . . .
it's time for you to see how positive interactions can do the same.

As in the first half of the exercise,
go over yesterday's personal interactions . . .
and find a pleasant one you had with a stranger . . .

It can be as simple as a smile . . .
holding a door or an elevator for someone . . .
or complimenting people on their appearance . . .

Once you have found a positive interaction with a stranger . . .
watch the whole thing happen again in your mind . . .
Pay attention to the tone your behavior set . . .

   ↪ *Pause 10 seconds.*

Did the other person register the constructive, supportive quality of
your act? . . .
Think about the way that person will pass along the positive feelings
you have encouraged to the next person he or she meets . . .

Perhaps that third person goes on to pass those feelings to
another . . .
Like a radio wave or a packet of energy,
this positive interaction that you created
bounces from one person to the next . . .
throughout the building . . . across town . . .
and conceivably around the globe.

Now search through yesterday's events for a positive interaction you
had with someone you know well . . .

You are going to put yourself in that person's place . . .
on the receiving end of the supportive action you made . . .

⮑ Pause 10 seconds.

Replay the event in detail . . .
Notice all the positive signals you gave off during the course
of your interaction . . .
perhaps a smile . . . a reassuring touch . . .
a slight raising of the eyebrows . . .
an encouraging tone of voice . . .

Each of these provokes a response,
a feeling of warmth, of security, of acceptance . . .

⮑ Pause 10 seconds.

Continuing in the role of your friend,
take those positive feelings with you to the next interaction . . .
Allow yourself to feel the desire to pass them along.

Perhaps this person is in a good mood too,
and you smile at each other . . .
Perhaps the next person looks downcast,
and you put a little extra effort into your greeting . . .

⮑ Pause 10 seconds.

Now let the chain reaction reach out to the present . . .
Feeling refreshed and renewed by the positive spirit . . .
Begin to become more consciously aware of your breathing . . .
more aware of yourself and others around you . . .

Take a deep breath and as you exhale, open your eyes . . .
and pass on the positive spirit.

GROUP PROCESSING OPTION

▨ Describe to a neighbor an instance when a stranger brightened
your day with a friendly word or considerate act. Then share insights
from your visualization experience.

HOMEWORK

▨ Make a conscious effort to relate positively to everyone you meet
on a given day. Notice the impact this has on others—and yourself.

Intimacy

Explore nonverbal, sensory connections to an intimate partner as you mentally affirm this special person.

GOAL

To increase enjoyment and appreciation of intimate relationships.

SPECIAL CONSIDERATIONS

Not appropriate for workplace settings. Extremely powerful for groups focused on relationship and intimacy issues, and for groups where all participants are in an intimate relationship with a special person.

Advance planning is necessary for the Variation, since participants will need to bring an object that enables them to concentrate on a special person.

WARMUP

When worries and responsibilities pile up, intimate relationships may become monotonous or automatic, rushed or perfunctory. Our schedule can hem us in, and the attention we give that special someone can become just another burden. We don't always take the time and care to fully enjoy and appreciate our partner.

In this exercise, you will take some time to learn (or re-learn) how special and wonderful an intimate relationship is. It may give you the opportunity to connect to a situation you've had in the past or to one you may want to have.

GUIDED IMAGE SCRIPT

Begin by exhaling and letting your eyes close . . .
Tune in to your innate sense of relaxation
and mental clarity . . .

With your eyes closed, simply listen to the words I speak . . .

I will be speaking words that might remind you of special events
and places where you might go for relaxation . . .

As I say the words . . .
get in touch with any associations you may have . . .
memories and experiences of true tranquillity . . . harmony . . .
and profound relaxation.

↝ *Read the list of places slowly.*

Beaches . . . waterbeds . . . rainbows . . . swings . . .
mountains . . . stars in the sky . . . waterfalls . . . lakes . . .
baths . . . sailing . . . forests . . . ponds . . . reading . . .
hot tubs . . . streams . . . cloud watching . . . movies . . .
daydreaming . . . couches . . . fishing . . . games . . . walks . . .
parks . . . meadows . . . music . . . food . . . weekends . . .
feeding birds . . . pets . . . bed . . . painting . . . hammocks . . .
flowers . . . kite flying . . . hugs . . . fireplaces . . . picnics . . .
balloons . . . floating . . . drifting . . . relaxing deeply.

Now within this state of profound relaxation,
think about your partner . . .
vividly bring to mind every detail . . .

Study his or her appearance . . .
and as you study how your partner looks in your mind,
allow a sense of comfort and relaxation to become a part of your
image . . .

↝ *Pause 15 seconds.*

Imagine yourself facing your partner . . .
standing ten feet away . . .

Neither speaks . . .
You merely look at each other at leisure and consider your feelings.

↝ *Pause 5 seconds.*

Soon, very slowly, the other person begins to move toward you . . .
Become intensely aware of how you feel
as the space between the two of you diminishes . . .

↝ *Pause 5 seconds.*

The other person approaches within seven feet . . .
and now five . . . filling more and more of your view . . .

⇐ Pause 5 seconds.

With much deliberation, your partner inches closer . . .
and both of you look at each other carefully . . .
The proximity increases bit by bit . . .
and you monitor your feelings
as this person approaches near enough to touch . . .

⇐ Pause 5 seconds.

Finally your partner stops moving . . .
but you do not touch each other . . .
nor do you speak . . .
You communicate and explore with your faces only . . .
moving your eyes . . . lips . . . brows . . . nose . . . facial
muscles . . . perhaps even tipping or turning your heads . . .

The two of you spend as much time as you need to find out what
you feel about each other . . .

⇐ Pause 15 seconds.

Now your partner's visit is finished . . .
You watch him or her return to the starting point . . .
ten feet away . . .

⇐ Pause 5 seconds.

Next, it is your turn to move and make the approach . . .

Slowly you walk toward the your partner . . .
Again, try to remain aware of all your feelings as you approach . . .
Watch the other person's face carefully
to catch any reactions to your movement . . .

⇐ Pause 5 seconds.

You move within five feet . . .
then two feet . . . perhaps even one foot away . . .

⇐ Pause 5 seconds.

Now you are very close to the other person . . .
but again you do not touch each other or talk . . .

Play with the space between the two of you . . .
Tip your body to the side to get a different perspective . . .
Rise up on your toes . . .
Sink down on your knees . . .
Lean your face in closer . . .

 ✑ *Pause 5 seconds.*

Always be aware of your feelings
throughout all these movements . . .
If any position does not feel right, make an adjustment . . .

 ✑ *Pause 5 seconds.*

Soon your visit is over . . .
Return to your spot at a ten-foot distance . . .
allowing all the emotions that have built up to dissipate . . .
and relax once more.

 ✑ *Pause 10 seconds.*

Now you and the other person are going to move simultaneously
toward each other . . .
Together you cut the distance between you . . .
slowly and with an awareness of your feelings . . .

 ✑ *Pause 5 seconds.*

When you have approached within arm's length,
both of you stop moving . . .
You stretch out your arms and communicate with your hands
only . . . without touching . . .
You look your partner in the face
but express how you feel with gestures . . .

Always allow yourself to remain aware of what you are feeling during
this encounter,
Notice whether it is all pleasurable . . .
or tinged with some doubt, fear, or apprehension . . .
Take as much time as you need to communicate fully
with your hands . . .

 ✑ *Pause 15 seconds.*

Now, while the person waits passively . . .
you are going to touch the other person's face with your hands . . .

Reach out and touch that cherished face . . .
Feel the many different textures of the face under your
fingertips . . .
Note the edges . . .
the soft depressions . . .
the points where extra heat may be detected . . .

As you explore the person's face with your hands,
remain aware of your feelings . . .
Note if the person smiles to communicate pleasure when you touch a
certain place or apply a certain caress . . .
Explore and caress for as long as you like . . .

 ↬ *Pause 10 seconds.*

When you have finished touching your partner's face . . .
it is your turn to sit passively
while your partner reaches out to touch your face . . .
Allow yourself to enjoy the sensations of that special person's fingers
as they play over the surfaces of your face . . .

While your partner explores your face . . .
try to read whatever emotions you can detect in that person's face and
eyes . . .
Without speaking, let the other person know which caresses give you
the most pleasure . . .

 ↬ *Pause 15 seconds.*

Now it's time to step back from this scene . . .

Allow your partner's face to fade away as you reflect upon your
experience . . .

And as you reflect,
you will drift back to the present and awaken.

 ↬ *Pause 5 seconds.*

When you are ready . . .
open your eyes . . .
stretch a bit . . .
and become aware of the other people around you.

GROUP PROCESSING OPTION

■ Pair up with someone you don't know well. Stand face to face, about two feet apart. The taller person should move forward or backward until you are at a comfortable distance *for you.*

■ Switch roles. Return to the two foot distance, and this time the shorter person should move forward or backward until you are at a comfortable distance *for you.*

■ Take a few minutes to debrief with the rest of the group. What did you learn about your level of intimacy in this setting?

HOMEWORK

■ Try out the exercise with a special person at home. Record the exercise on tape first so you can play it at home and concentrate fully on the experience.

VARIATION

■ To prepare for this visualization, ask participants to bring an object that will enable them to concentrate on their special person: a photo, a piece of clothing, or a bottle of perfume or cologne. Modify the script in a manner similar to *Picture*, page 104, to incorporate the use of props.

Raising a Child

Discover hidden strengths as you visualize the rich dynamics of parent-child relationships at several stages of life.

GOAL

To increase awareness of parent-child dynamics and to connect with your inner child.

TIME

8–10 minutes

SPECIAL CONSIDERATIONS

Ideal for parenting groups or for couples who are considering having a child. Also useful for groups of people who work with children.

To get warmed up for this experience, participants could visit a nursery school, day care center, park, or other location where they can closely observe a small child. Or the group leader could show a brief film or video of small children as preparation for the exercise.

⤸ *Be sure to have the appropriate A-V equipment set up in advance. The screen size should be large enough for all to see easily.*

WARMUP

▨ Whether or not you intend to raise a child, you may learn a lot from this exercise.

▨ Through this image, you can acquire a greater appreciation for your parents and the responsibility they took in raising you. In addition, you will see how taking on such a responsibility means you have to make an honest assessment of yourself—strengths, weaknesses, personality, and values.

▨ Finally, you can be nourished and grow from this opportunity to share the perceptions and exuberance of a child.

GUIDED IMAGE SCRIPT

To prepare for this visualization, think back on your own childhood and the process of growing up . . . the high and low points . . . the exciting activities . . . and the burdens.

Take a few moments to remember.

 ↜ *Pause 15 seconds.*

Now settle back comfortably . . . and in the quiet of your mind . . . relax and reflect on your memories and observations.
As you do . . . feel your body relax and your eyes close.

 ↜ *Pause 15 seconds.*

You are fully relaxed . . .
breathing easily from your belly like a newborn baby.

Imagine yourself in the maternity ward of a hospital . . .
The nurse has just handed you your newborn baby . . .
Take a few moments to absorb what has happened
and realize that this baby is actually a part of you . . .

Observe the baby closely . . . noticing your reactions as you observe its face . . . hands . . . fingers . . . toes . . . skin . . . hair . . .
Drink in the sight of this precious child . . .

 ↜ *Pause 10 seconds.*

Now, thanking the nurse and doctors for their care,
take your infant home . . .

Once you have come home, take time to study this newborn creature . . . Notice its appearance . . . the wispy hair on its huge but fragile head . . . its jerky movements and soft skin . . . the total helplessness . . . Notice any likeness to you . . .
and reflect on how you might have looked as a child . . .

 ↜ *Pause 15 seconds.*

Take note also of your feelings as you look upon the tiny bundle in your care . . . Be aware of your demeanor . . .
and the language you use if you speak to the infant . . .
Then, when the baby goes to sleep . . . you go to sleep as well . . .

 ↜ *Pause 15 seconds.*

When you wake up, you will find that three years have passed . . .
You go into the child's room and notice how he or she has
grown . . . Aside from the physical changes . . . observe any more
subtle signs of the passage of time . . . By now, the child has a good
grasp on the rudiments of language, and you pay attention to every
word spoken . . . Imagine what your three-year-old would say . . .

  ᴥ *Pause 15 seconds.*

Now, you decide to take your three-year-old on an outing . . .
The two of you take a walk to the park . . . or to a country
setting . . . Watch how your child reacts to the world . . .
What questions does your child ask . . . and how do you respond?

As you interact with your child,
try to assess the personality traits you observe . . .
Undoubtedly, your child will have drawn some of its character from
you . . . but some traits may play off against yours . . .

Again, watch how you tailor your demeanor . . .
and the language you use
now that your child has grown beyond the nonverbal stage.

  ᴥ *Pause 15 seconds.*

The fresh air makes you both hungry, and you decide to eat . . .
It is a pleasure to watch your child eat with such gusto! . . .
Then, pleasantly weary from a long day's jaunt,
the two of you return home and go to sleep . . .

  ᴥ *Pause 5 seconds.*

When you next awaken . . .
the child is six years old and attending school . . .
On this particular afternoon,
you have agreed to help your child learn to ride a bike . . .
After returning home from school,
the six-year-old pulls out the little bicycle for a lesson . . .
For awhile you run alongside or behind the bike
and hold it upright as your child pedals along . . .
It is exhausting work . . .
and you find yourself breathing very hard to keep up . . .
At certain moments you let go of the bicycle for an instant
and watch your child pedal ahead . . .

You observe the child either toppling over . . . or putting feet down to keep from falling . . . Notice whether you feel confidence and hope each time you see this . . . or apprehension and pity . . .

Finally, on one occasion, you let go . . . and your child wobbles uncertainly but rides all the way to the end of the block . . .

You watch the little bicycle travel to the corner . . . stop . . . wheel around . . . and come back . . . all under your child's control . . .

Your child is exuberant, and it's a good moment for the two of you . . . although you realize that riding a bike is now one of the things your child will no longer need your help to do . . .

Tired from all your running, you walk into the house and lie down to rest . . . Reflect upon your feelings . . . about the fact that your child has mastered this new skill . . . before you fall asleep . . .

     ⌐ *Pause 15 seconds.*

This time when you arise, your child has attained the age of sixteen years . . . You can see dramatic physical changes in your teenager's body . . . and strong mood swings . . .
Your child has entered the emotional world of adults, and met his or her first love . . . Tonight your sixteen-year-old is going on a dinner date with this special person . . .

There is much fanfare and excitement over the preparations, and your child turns to you for suggestions for clothing and on how to behave . . .

As you offer your advice, notice your feelings about your child and this rite of adolescence . . .

A conflict develops over the issue of what time you expect your teenager to be home . . . For a dinner date, you suggest that ten o'clock is not unrealistic, but your child lobbies strongly for midnight . . . The argument threatens to become hurtful, but the two of you work out an agreeable compromise . . .
Then your teen-ager leaves the house for the big date . . .

Reflect upon your first love and the trials of growing up . . .
Think about what is happening to your child at this age . . .

and what changes have occurred since ages three and six . . .

Pause 15 seconds.

Now, make an assessment . . .
what kind of job do you think you have done as a parent?
What interests, skills, and talents does this child of yours possess?
Is your child introverted, or more of an extrovert? . . .
How did that happen? . . .
Perhaps some aspects of your child's personality have developed
despite your best wishes . . . outside of your control . . .
How does or did that happen?

Pause 15 seconds.

While you have been ruminating, your teen-ager has been enjoying a
fine evening out . . . Not surprisingly, the child gets home a little
later than the time the two of you had agreed upon . . . but no harm
has been done. You issue a friendly warning and send your teen-ager
happily to bed . . .

Now that your child is safely home and asleep, you acknowledge that
this has only been an image . . . a projection of your own fears . . .
strengths . . . and desires . . .

Reflect on what you've seen . . .
the creation of a separate life that shares attributes with yours . . .

Pause 15 seconds.

When you have considered your work to your satisfaction . . .
open your eyes and come back to this room . . .
bringing what you have learned back with you . . .
to the present time.

GROUP PROCESSING OPTION

Share with others in the group what your parenting experience
was like in the visualization. Be sure to share both positive and
negative feelings.

*As people share, connect their experiences and point
out common themes.*

Chapter 12

RESOURCES

TIPS FOR GROUP LEADERS:
ENHANCING IMAGES WITH SENSORY AWARENESS

Visualization is not just a visual process. All five senses can be used to channel imagery experiences and relaxation responses. Usually individuals have stronger input from one or two sensory modalities. Some people receive more sensory information from seeing or hearing, others from taste, smell, or touch. Often people will remember an entire evening from the distant past, simply by smelling a waft of cigar smoke or a certain perfume. People who are skilled with their hands usually receive most sensory information through kinesthetic or tactile stimulation, while others may have most of their memory attached to sounds and sights.

All of the scripts in this book incorporate two or more dimensions of sensory exploration. Some call on all five senses. Since each person in your group may have different sensory strengths, you will want to enhance any guided image with as many sensory modalities as possible.

As you become more and more comfortable with leading relaxation and guided imagery, you may want to incorporate even more sensory stimulation into your visualization. Feel free to expand the scripts with any of the suggestions below.

■ RELAXING THROUGH SIGHT. Subdued and soft lighting is the most conducive for relaxing and imaging. During daylight hours, shades or drapes can be drawn to eliminate glare. At night the indoor lighting should be kept low.

Pay attention to the colors in your environment. Colors create moods and influence our perceptions and behaviors. Warm colors such as red, orange, and yellow are stimulating, but may provoke agitation or fatigue, which hinder relaxation. Cool tones, such as blue and green, are more likely to generate a restful, relaxed response

■ RELAXING THROUGH SOUND. Several auditory tools can enhance relaxation and visualization. Environmental sounds, such as the surf, an approaching thunderstorm, wind in the trees, or a babbling brook can be very powerful mood setters that aid the imaging process. A metronome, water slowly dripping, or subtle instrumental music makes a good relaxation accompaniment. Some people prefer a totally silent room.

■ RELAXING THROUGH TOUCH. Massage and stretching are the most direct tactile relaxants. For maximum sensory input, you might want to use a stretching or massage script as the relaxing prelude to an imagery script that evokes other senses.

We don't often think about our internal tactile sensations, but the lining of the digestive tract is composed of the same type of highly sensitive cells as our skin. Trying to relax and image on an empty stomach, or a full one, can be distracting. Drinking a warm liquid (tea, milk, cider) has a direct, soothing effect on the throat and stomach, and is likely to enhance the overall relaxation effect.

Experiment with adding tactile exploration to all your images. For example, "Mentally explore your safe haven; notice the temperatures and textures around you; are the walls rough or smooth? Is the floor cool or warm? Reach out and touch an inviting surface, explore it with your fingertips."

Try to maintain a comfortable, steady temperature during guided imagery. Excessive cold may cause your body to tense, while a very hot room is equally uncomfortable. Avoid sudden changes you can control—such as drafts, fans, or open windows.

RELAXING THROUGH SMELL AND TASTE. Our olfactory processes are a surprisingly useful tool for enhancing visualization and relaxation. Aromatherapy utilizes certain basic or mixed scents designed to appeal to many of the body's chemical reactions. You may want to experiment on your own with bottled relaxation aromas (chamomile, basil, sage, etc.) from the health foods store, but be cautious about using actual scents with a group. Many people are highly sensitive to odors and can have severe allergic reactions.

Fortunately, imagination is nearly as powerful as reality. Add some vivid aromatic imagery to your scripts and participants' mental noses will breathe it in.

Our sense of taste is closely tied to our sense of smell, and our mental tastebuds are nearly as powerful as our physical ones. Where appropriate, enhance your visualization with invitations to recall certain flavors or to taste the images themselves.

On a more practical note, a glass of water before any imagery session may prevent the "cotton mouth" feeling which often accompanies deep states of relaxation.

TIPS FOR GROUP LEADERS:
MUSIC FOR RELAXATION AND IMAGERY

Accompanying music should support the relaxation and imaging process, not disrupt it.

When choosing music for relaxation, look for unfamiliar, soothing pieces with a slow tempo and no discernible melody or pattern. A single instrument in the middle range (e.g., piano, harp, cello, guitar, oboe) is usually better than a busy symphonic piece or any instrument in a very high register.

Some of the classics work well for relaxation, and several inexpensive collections for this purpose are available in music stores. Choose *largo, andante,* or *adagio* sections. Stay away from familiar pieces which might distract music lovers who mentally anticipate the unfolding composition rather than attending to their internal imagery process.

Many people prefer the wandering, melody-less style of new age or "space" music for relaxation. Whether generated by acoustic piano or synthesizer, this music seems to invite daydreaming.

Steven Halpern, author of *Sound Health,* and one of the pioneer composers of this type of music, has researched extensively the positive relaxation effects of his *anti-frantic* compositions. His *Comfort Zone* and *Spectrum Suite* albums are particularly soothing. Many of the Windham Hill artists have followed in Halpern's footsteps. Steve Eckels' *musical prayers for healing* on classical guitar evoke the same type of calming, altered state of consciousness.

To enhance particular visualization experiences, you may want to choose music that evokes specific images or feelings—Debussy's *La Mer,* for example, or the mournful tones of a Russian folk tune played on the balalaika.

Consult the list of music sources on page 235 to find appropriate recordings for relaxation and imaging.

TIPS FOR GROUP LEADERS:
OVERCOMING TENSION AND RESISTANCE

Each experience leading guided imagery will offer its own challenges. As a leader, you need to be prepared to handle several common situations.

DISTURBING IMAGES. At the beginning of every session, remind group members that *they* are in control of the imagery experience and should trust their own instincts. There is no need to suffer unpleasant or upsetting images. Encourage participants to shift their attention from the disturbing image to their breathing, or to a more pleasant image of their own choosing. If necessary, they can just open their eyes and discontinue the imaging process.

Always give individuals in the group a non-participation option. Never insist that people close their eyes or join the imaging process. Those who just "listen in" without actively participating may be gaining benefits at their own level.

If any of the images in the visualization scripts are at all disturbing to group members, simply move on to another image.

One word of caution to all leaders not trained in psychiatric therapies:

relaxation techniques and guided imagery are not appropriate tools for severely mentally ill patients. If someone should "freak out" or slip into a hallucinating state, calm reassurance and reality-based conversation is usually the best strategy.

▌**TENSION.** Tension interferes with relaxation and visualization. Group tension, physical discomfort, and mental strain can all obstruct the open mind which is necessary for guided imagery to be effective.

An ounce of prevention is worth a pound of cure. Be sure to help the group relax fully before beginning guided imagery. Do not skip or minimize this essential component.

▌**DIFFICULTY "SEEING" THE VISUALIZATIONS.** Some of your group members will probably experience some difficulty visualizing the images you are reading to them. Part of your job as a facilitator is to enrich these images so that every member can *see* the image.

Slowing your pace and adding evocative sensory images will usually help. For example, "Allow yourself to feel the warmth of the sun beating down on your face, baking your skin, and penetrating all the way down to your bones," or "Take a moment to drink in your surroundings . . . What sounds do you hear? What smells do you notice?"

Encourage people to go with the flow, even if they do not seem able to picture the images exactly. Remind them that visualization is a skill—with practice their imaging capacity will increase. For some, a quick reassurance that their unconscious is getting the message, even if they cannot *see* it, may be needed.

Your confidence that the process is working will be contagious. The synergy of the group often carries along the nonbeliever and often stimulates visualization for people who have difficulty imaging.

▌**RESPONDING TO EMOTIONAL REACTIONS.** Most newcomers to guided imagery in groups worry about what might happen if someone gets extremely emotional during a visualization. Instead of panicking, rejoice. Such displays are sure indicators that the imagery is working!

Be sure you tell every group during your warmup about the possibility of painful memories being triggered by visualizations—and about the potential for healing and growth that accompanies such deep discoveries.

If anyone in the group experiences intense emotional pain during a visualization, stay calm. Remember that strong emotions are one of the desirable healthy by-products of effective imagery.

Show respect for the person's privacy by allowing silence or time and space for the person to cry and process the feelings without intrusive attention. Quietly offer a tissue and continue reading the script. Keep the pace moving.

If the person's reaction persists after the imaging is finished, get the group started on its own processing exercise and then approach the individual, kneel or sit beside him or her, and quietly ask, "Are you okay? I don't want to interfere, but is there anything I can do to help?" You might ask if a gentle, comforting touch, such as an arm around the shoulder, a pat or reassuring squeeze on the arm would be appreciated.

Encourage people with emotional reactions to talk about them with a partner or small group. Giving words to feelings often leads to powerful insights. The group can also be a tremendous support resource. Ask others in the group who have had similar emotional reactions in the past or present to share a bit about their experiences.

Compliment individuals for their courage to share in the group. Affirm everyone for their willingness to try the visualizations, and for their openness to new possibilities for growth. Remind the group about confidentiality and how important this is to maintain trust in the group.

If sharing in the group is not appropriate, encourage the individual to take the time she or he needs to regain composure while you make a bridge to the next agenda item or move to a new discussion question.

TIPS FOR GROUP LEADERS:
WORKING WITH AN ONGOING GROUP

If you are leading an ongoing group or guided imagery class, you will want to structure the experience differently from a single guided imagery session.

■ **GROUP GROUND RULES.** Group dynamics are even more powerful in an extended group experience, so you will want to pay special attention to setting appropriate ground rules about participation, levels of self-disclosure, and confidentiality. Group processing of images will be a rich source of learning for everyone.

■ **REFLECTION TOOLS.** Experiment with different reflection processes—totally private mental rumination; extended personal reflection in writing; processing in pairs briefly; processing in depth with a partner, trio, or small group; sharing briefly or at length with the whole group; reading written reflections aloud; creating new imagery together; practicing leading the imaging process with a partner or group; keeping an imaging log or dream journal; using a between-sessions buddy system—the possibilities for insight and growth are abundant.

■ **SEQUENCING.** At the beginning of the course, you may want to spend several sessions on relaxation techniques, with between-session practice assignments so that everyone explores enough options to find one that suits. Then continue subsequent meetings by using different guided images and processing techniques with the group. After a session or two of visualization, encourage participants to help choose images for the next session, based on their individual needs and issues.

■ **CLOSURE.** During the final session, be sure to include some kind of positive closure experience for the group, such as an imagery experience that affirms each member in turn. By this time the group should be comfortable enough to create its own closing ritual.

■ **HOMEWORK.** Take advantage of time between sessions to assign appropriate homework—relaxation practice, self-guided visualization exercises, journal-keeping, interviewing people about their relaxation patterns and favorite images, and supporting other class members.

Resources on Guided Imagery

Achterberg, Jeanne, Barbara Dossey, and Leslie Kolkmeier. *Rituals of Healing.* New York: Bantam Books, 1994.

Adair, Margo. *Working Inside Out: Tools for Change.* Berkeley CA: Wingbow Press, 1984.

Benjamin, Harold. *From Victim to Victor.* New York: Dell Publishing, 1989.

Dass, Ram. *Journey of Awakening.* New York: Bantam Books, 1978.

Emery, Marcia. *Intuition Workbook: An Expert's Guide to Unlocking the Wisdom of Your Subconscious Mind.* New York: Prentice Hall, 1994.

Erickson, Milton and E.L. Rossi. *Hypnotic Realities.* New York: Irvington Publishers, Inc., 1979.

Fanning, Patrick. *Visualization for Change.* Oakland CA: New Harbinger Publications, Inc., 1988.

Fezler, W. *Imagery for Healing, Knowledge, and Power: Harnessing Your Personal Energy to Create.* New York: Fireside Publishing, 1990.

Gawain, Shakti. *Creative Visualizations.* San Rafael CA: New World Library, 1978.

Gawain, Shakti. *Meditations: Creative Visualization and Meditation Exercises to Enrich Your Life.* San Rafael CA: New World Library, 1991.

Kravette, Steve. *Complete Meditation.* Rockport MA: Para Research, 1982.

Kravette, Steve. *Complete Relaxation.* Rockport MA: Para Research, 1979.

Luce, Gay G. *Longer Life, More Joy: Techniques for Enhancing Health, Happiness, and Inner Vision.* North Hollywood CA: Newcastle Publishing, 1992.

Lusk, Julie T. *30 Scripts for Relaxation and Inner Healing.* Duluth MN: Whole Person Associates Inc., 1993.

Masters, Robert and Jean Houston. *Mind Games.* New York: Dell Publishing, 1973.

Naparstek, Belleruth. *Staying Well with Guided Imagery.* New York: Warner Books, 1994.

Pierrakos, Eva. *The Pathwork of Self-Transformations.* New York: Bantam Books, 1990.

Progoff, Ira. *The Practice of Process Meditation.* New York: Dialogue House, 1980.

Rossman, Martin. *Healing Yourself: A Step-by-Step Program for Better Health Through Imagery.* New York: Simon & Schuster, 1994.

Samuels, Mike and Nancy Samuels. *Seeing with the Mind's Eye.* New York: Random House, 1975.

Satir, Virginia. *Meditations and Inspirations.* Berkeley CA: Celestial Arts, 1985.

Siegel, Bernie. *Love, Medicine, and Miracles.* New York: Harper & Row, 1986.

Schwartz, Stephen. *Visualizations: Breaking through the Illusion of Problems.* Piermont NY: River Run Press, 1985.

Schwartz, Andrew E. *Inquire Within: 24 Visualizations for Creativity & Growth.* Duluth MN: Whole Person Associates Inc., 1993.

Zilbergeld, Bernie and Lazarus. *Mind Power: Getting What You Want through Mental Training.* New York: Ivy Books, 1988.

Zukav, Gary. *The Seat of the Soul.* New York: Fireside, 1989.

MUSIC SOURCES

If you have difficulty finding appropriate recorded music locally, write or call for catalogs from these specialists in new age or relaxation music.

Celestial Harmonies. 4549 E Fort Lowell, Tucson AZ 85712. (602) 326–4400.

Global Pacific Records. 1275 E MacArthur St, Sonoma CA 95476. (707) 996–2748.

Halpern Sounds. PO Box 2644, San Anselmo CA 94960. Dozens of titles from the relaxation pioneer.

Music Design. 4650 N Port Washington Rd, Milwaukee WI 53212. (414) 961–8380. Large distributor of alternative music.

Narada Productions Inc. 4650 N Port Washington Rd, Milwaukee WI 53212. (414) 961–8350.

New Leaf Distributing. 5425 Tulane Dr SW, Atlanta GA 30336. (404) 691–6996. One of the largest distributors of new age books and tapes. Wholesale only, no direct sales, but they will help you locate a nearby retailer.

Private Music. 9014 Melrose Ave, Los Angeles CA 90069. (213) 859–9200.

Real Music. 85 Libertyship, Sausalito CA 94965. (213) 859–9200.

Rykodisc. 530 N 3rd St, Minneapolis MN 55401. (612) 375–9162.

Sounding of the Planet. PO Box 43512, Tucson AZ 85733. (602) 792–9888.

Synchestra. PO Box 915, Camden ME 04843. (207) 594–5657.

Whole Person Press. 210 W Michigan St, Duluth MN 55802. (800) 247–6789. Steven Halpern and Steve Eckels music, plus many unusual guided images on tape.

Windham Hill Productions Inc, PO Box 9388, Stanford CA 94305. (415) 329–0647. The best-known publisher of new age music by many artists.

Guided Imagery Books
by Andrew Schwartz

Inquire Within

Andrew Schwartz

Use visualization to help people make positive changes in their life. The 24 visualization experiences in *Inquire Within* will help participants enhance their creativity, heal inner pain, learn to relax, and deal with conflict. Each visualization includes questions at the end of the process that encourage deeper reflection and a better understanding of the exercise and the response it evokes.

Inquire Within / $19.95

Companion audiotapes: ■ *Healing Visions* ■ *Relaxing Retreats*

Guided Imagery for Groups

Andrew Schwartz

Ideal for courses, workshops, team building, and personal stress management, this comprehensive resource includes scripts for 50 thematic visualizations that promote calming, centering, creativity, congruence, clarity, coping, and connectedness. Detailed instructions for using relaxation techniques and guided images in group settings allow educators at all levels, in any setting, to help people tap into the healing and creative powers of imagery.

Guided Imagery for Groups / $24.95

Companion audiotapes: ■ *Healing Visions* ■ *Relaxing Retreats*

Guided Imagery Audiotapes

Take a Deep Breath

Tension relief is as simple as breathing when your breathing is accompanied by guided imagery. When you need to unwind, sit back and do what comes naturally— breathe. Electric piano background by Steven Halpern. Adapted from Julie Lusk's *30 Scripts for Relaxation, Imagery & Inner Healing.*

Breathing for Relaxation and Health 14:00 • The Magic Ball 17:00

Take a Deep Breath / $11.95

Refreshing Journeys

This imagery sampler provides a powerful introduction to guided imagery and its potential for stress management and enhancing well-being. Classical guitar background by Steve Eckels. Adapted from Julie Lusk's *30 Scripts for Relaxation, Imagery & Inner Healing.*

**1 to 10 10:00 • Thoughts Library 11:00 • Visualizing Change 7:00
Magic Carpet 10:00 • Pond of Love 10:00 • Cruise 9:00**

Refreshing Journeys / $11.95

Healing Visions

Guided imagery is a powerful source for renewal and healing. These six images will restore balance and well-being. Classical guitar background by Steve Eckels. Adapted from Andrew Schwartz' *Guided Imagery for Groups* and *Inquire Within.*

**Rocking Chair 6:00 • Pine Forest 12:00 • Long Lost Confidant 11:00
Caterpillar to Butterfly 10:00 • Superpowers 10:00 • Tornado 12:00**

Healing Visions / $11.95

Relaxing Retreats

Six opportunities for letting go of tension and creating inner peace—all through the power of your imagination. Electric piano background by Steven Halpern. Adapted from Andrew Schwartz' *Guided Imagery for Groups* and *Inquire Within.*

Melting Candle 5:00 • Tropical Paradise 11:00 • Sanctuary 9:00
Floating Clouds 5:00 • Seasons 10:00 • Beach Tides 14:00

 **Relaxing Retreats / $11.95**

Music for Relaxation

Beautiful, original music that can be played as background to a prepared guided imagery script—or simply enjoyed as a way to calm your body, mind, and spirit. These performances are adaptable to any environment, adding a warm and nurturing ambiance without imposing specific demands on the listener.

Steven Eckels

Classical guitarist Eckels draws inspiration from Gregorian chant, Native American melodies, the rhythms of Lake Superior and the spirit of the North Woods in composing his *musical prayers for healing.*

Tranquility / $11.95　　Serenity / $11.95　　Harmony / $11.95

Steven Halpern

Halpern is internationally acclaimed for his use of *anti-frantic* music to promote health and well-being. The free-floating nature of his electric and grand piano music triggers a delightful state of relaxation and enjoyment.

Comfort Zone / $11.95　　Spectrum Suite / $11.95

RELAXATION RESOURCES

*To order
call toll free*
(800) 247-6789

About Whole Person Associates

At Whole Person Associates, we're 100% committed to providing stress and wellness materials that involve participants and provide a "whole person" focus—body, mind, spirit, and relationships.

About the Owners

Whole Person Associates was created by the vision of two people: Donald A. Tubesing, PhD, and Nancy Loving Tubesing, EdD. Don and Nancy have been active in the stress management/wellness promotion movement for over twenty years—consulting, leading seminars, writing, and publishing. Most of our early products were the result of their creativity and expertise. Living proof that you can "stay evergreen," Don and Nancy remain the driving force behind the company and are still active in developing new products that touch people's lives.

About the Company

Whole Person Associates was "born" in Duluth, Minnesota, and we remain committed to our lovely city on the shore of Lake Superior. We put the same high quality into every product we offer, translating the best of current research into practical, accessible, easy-to-use materials. We create the best possible resources to help our customers teach about stress management and wellness promotion. And our friendly and resourceful employees are committed to helping you find the products that fit your needs.

About our Associates

Who are the "associates" in Whole Person Associates? They're the trainers, authors, musicians, and others who have developed much of the material you see on these pages. We're always on the lookout for high-quality products that reflect our "whole person" philosophy and fill a need for our customers. Our products were developed by experts who are at the top of their fields, and we're very proud to be associated with them.

About our Relationship to You

We'd love to hear from you! Let us know what you think of our products—how you use them in your work, what additional products you'd like to see, and what shortcomings you've noted. Write us or call on our toll-free line. We look forward to hearing from you!